GREAT DISCOVERIES IN SCIENCE

Quantum Mechanics

Kate Shoup

Cavendish
Square

New York

Published in 2019 by Cavendish Square Publishing, LLC
243 5th Avenue, Suite 136, New York, NY 10016

Copyright © 2019 by Cavendish Square Publishing, LLC

First Edition

Website: cavendishsq.com

Library of Congress Cataloging-in-Publication Data

Names: Shoup, Kate, 1972- author.
Title: Quantum mechanics / Kate Shoup.
Description: First edition. | New York, NY : Cavendish Square Publishing,
[2019] | Series: Great discoveries in science | Includes bibliographical
references and index. | Audience: 9 to 12.
Identifiers: LCCN 2018009491 (print) | LCCN 2018025895 (ebook) |
ISBN 9781502643728 (ebook) | ISBN 9781502643827 (library bound) | | ISBN 9781502643940 (pbk.)
Subjects: LCSH: Quantum theory--History--Juvenile literature. |
Physics--History. | Physicists--Juvenile literature.
Classification: LCC QC173.98 (ebook) | LCC QC173.98 .S56 2019 (print) | DDC 530.12--dc23
LC record available at https://lccn.loc.gov/2018009491

Editorial Director: David McNamara
Editor: Jodyanne Benson
Copy Editor: Michele Suchomel-Casey
Associate Art Director: Alan Sliwinski
Designer: Christina Shults
Production Coordinator: Karol Szymczuk
Photo Research: J8 Media

Printed in the United States of America

Contents

Top quantum physicists attend a 1927 meeting, including Erwin Schrödinger (*back row, center*), Wolfgang Pauli (*back row, fourth from right*), Werner Heisenberg (*back row, third from right*), Paul Dirac (*middle row, second from left*), Louis de Broglie (*middle row, third from right*), Niels Bohr (*middle row, far right*), Max Planck (*front row, second from left*), Marie Curie (*front row, third from left*), and Albert Einstein (*front row, center*).

Introduction

In 1900, an eminent scientist named Lord Kelvin (1824–1907) addressed a gathering of the British Association for the Advancement of Science. "There is nothing new to be discovered in physics now," he told his audience. "All that remains is more and more precise measurement." This seemed a perfectly reasonable statement for the time.

For thousands of years humans had strived to understand the inner workings of our world. At first, they explained various natural phenomena by appealing to mythology or religion. Later they developed a practice of scientific inquiry (which came to be called physics) to describe them. During the 1600s, a scientist named Sir Isaac Newton seemed to settle the matter of how our world works once and for all. He published a book that outlined three laws of motion and a law of gravity. These laws, which described a universe that operated as predictably as a mechanical clock, survived more than two hundred years of scrutiny by members of the scientific community.

As it turned out, however, Lord Kelvin could not have been more wrong. Within a matter of months, a German scientist named Max Planck would make a revolutionary discovery that would herald an entirely new understanding of physics. Indeed, this discovery, called quantum physics or quantum mechanics, would eventually replace classical physics (also called Newtonian physics) altogether—at least in the study of microscopic particles. (The principles of classical physics do still largely apply to the macroscopic world.)

For the most part, quantum physicists concern themselves with very small things—namely, atoms and photons. But what they've learned about these very small things has enormous implications. Indeed, quantum physics has become, in the words of Nobel laureate Steven Weinberg, "the basis of our understanding of not only atoms, but also atomic nuclei, electrical conduction, magnetism, electromagnetic radiation, semiconductors, superconductors, white dwarf stars, neutron stars, nuclear forces and elementary particles."

This did not happen all at once. Several scientists worked tirelessly to achieve this—each providing their own blocks upon which future scientists would build. Max Planck (1858–1947) discovered that energy is emitted in short bursts rather than continuously. Albert Einstein (1885–1962) confirmed Planck's discovery and conceived a new way to describe light. Niels Bohr (1885–1962) developed a new quantum model of the atom. Louis de Broglie (1892–1987) concluded that like light, all matter has wave properties. Max Born (1882–1970) conceived a way to describe the wave characteristics of a particle in mathematical terms. Erwin Schrödinger (1887–1961) formulated an equation to calculate the energy level of an electron in an atom.

Wolfgang Pauli (1900–1958) observed that no two electrons in an atom can occupy the same quantum state at the same time. Werner Heisenberg (1901–1976) asserted that it is impossible to measure both the position and the momentum of a quantum at the same time. Paul Dirac (1902–1984) formulated an equation to describe the behavior of certain subatomic particles.

Scientists have since discovered many applications for quantum physics. These have resulted in the advancement of several important technologies, such as the laser, magnetic resonance imaging (MRI), the Global Positioning System (GPS), nuclear fission, and the transistor. All these technologies—particularly nuclear fission and the transistor—have transformed our societies. Other technologies in development—particularly quantum computing and quantum cryptography—promise yet more change.

Interestingly, although quantum physics has proved to be remarkably accurate, it also possesses what many scientists called an "inherent weirdness." In other words, the rules of quantum physics often seem counterintuitive or even flat-out wrong. For example, quantum physics dictates that light and matter exhibit a quality called wave-particle duality. Wave-particle duality is when something behaves like both waves and particles.

Quantum physics also asserts that the universe is fundamentally random. But there are even weirder aspects to quantum physics, like superposition (which allows a quantum to exist in two positions or states at once), quantum entanglement (in which one quantum can affect the position or state of another quantum even from a tremendous distance), and quantum tunneling (by which particles "tunnel" through the membrane of a nucleus even though they lack sufficient energy to do so). The strangeness of these propositions has led many scientists—including Einstein and Schrödinger, whose contributions to the field were significant—to reject quantum physics entirely.

There are also problems with quantum physics that have not yet been solved. These problems could indicate one of three things: that our understanding of quantum physics is wrong; that our understanding of quantum physics is correct but incomplete; or that these problems aren't problems at all because quantum physics is abstract in nature, rather than rooted in reality and what we can observe with our senses. While some scientists ponder these issues at great length, others seem to ignore them altogether, taking the approach of using formulas and calculations.

Either way, the effects of quantum physics on the science world—indeed the world at large—have been enormous. To understand the underpinnings of this exciting and evolving field, read on!

Lasers are one of many inventions
that came from research in
quantum mechanics.

This fresco in Perugia, Italy, depicts the Greek god Apollo. The ancient Greeks believed Apollo towed the sun across the sky behind his chariot each day.

CHAPTER 1

From Classical Physics to the Modern Era

For thousands of years, humans have sought to understand the world around them. Over time that thirst for understanding evolved into the scientific discipline called physics.

PHYSICS in ANCIENT TIMES

In their attempt to understand the natural world, early humans turned to mythology, religion, or the supernatural realm to answer questions like what the world was made of, where the sun went at night, and so on. For example, members of most early societies believed that one or more gods created the world. The Navajos believed a god named Tsohanoai hauled the sun across the sky on his back during the day and hung it on a peg inside his home at night. The ancient Greeks and Egyptians shared a similar belief—only their gods hitched the sun to a chariot and a boat, respectively.

A shift in thinking occurred during the Archaic period (650–480 BCE) in ancient Greece. Greek scholars continued to worship their pantheon of gods, but they began to take a more rational approach to understanding the natural world. That is to say, they carefully observed it and applied these observations to formulate hypotheses and theories about its inner workings. This practice, which the Greeks called *physis* (meaning "nature"), is the earliest incarnation of physics as we know it today.

Some hypotheses and theories put forth by the ancient Greeks seem strange today. For example, Aristotle (384–322 BCE) believed that all matter was composed of earth, water, air, and fire, rather than chemical elements. (To be fair, Aristotle had plenty of perfectly plausible ideas, too. For example, Aristotle forwarded the notion that "continuation of motion depends on continued action of a force," which held for more than a millennium. He also developed a series of standard techniques for scientific inquiry.)

Other ancient Greek hypotheses and theories, however, seem almost astonishing in their accuracy. For example, the ancient Greeks concluded Earth was spherical, determined that it rotated on an axis, and calculated both its circumference and its distance from the sun and the moon. They also suggested (though never proved) that the solar system was heliocentric—meaning Earth revolved around the sun rather than the other way around. The ancient Greeks even mapped the motion of several stars and planets and deduced how to predict solar eclipses.

MEDIEVAL SCHOLARSHIP

In 146 BCE, the Roman Empire absorbed the Greek Empire. More than six hundred years later, in 476 CE, the Roman Empire collapsed. Chaos engulfed the Western Roman Empire in western Europe. During this period, much of the advanced scientific knowledge gleaned by the ancient Greeks was lost. Indeed, as far as medieval western Europeans knew, Earth was flat, the sun revolved around it, and events such as solar eclipses were the result of divine intervention by the Christian god. (Some principles of Aristotelian physics, including his views on the composition of matter and on the nature of motion, survived.)

This knowledge was not lost everywhere, however. Citizens of the Byzantine Empire (formerly the Eastern Roman Empire) guarded volumes of scientific texts written by the ancient Greeks. Later, Muslim scholars throughout Byzantium—which comprised the Balkan Peninsula in eastern Europe, modern-day Turkey, parts of central Asia and the Middle East, and northern Africa—translated these texts into Arabic and built on the knowledge they imparted.

Between 1095 and 1291, the Roman Catholic Church, headquartered in Rome, launched a series of assaults on the Byzantine Empire called the Crusades. One unexpected result of this ongoing campaign was that it exposed European crusaders to a wealth of desirable goods from the East—from spices to silks to carpets to cotton and beyond. This in turn led to increased trade between Europe and Byzantium. The Europeans and the Byzantines didn't just

Roger Bacon was a philosopher and Franciscan friar who supported experimental science during the medieval era.

trade goods, however. They traded knowledge too, including the scientific knowledge put forth by the ancient Greeks and guarded by the Byzantines.

Slowly, this scientific knowledge trickled back to Europe. As it did, European scholars worked feverishly to reconcile it with Christian theology. (Naturally, when faced with contradictions—and there were many—these scholars inevitably acceded to the Christian view.) In 1453, when the Ottoman Empire conquered Byzantium, Byzantine intellectuals fled west, and the trickle of knowledge became a flood.

The effect of this flood was two-fold. First, it ushered in an era of incredible scientific discovery by European scholars, called the Scientific Revolution. Second—and perhaps more important—it introduced European scholars to the Greek method of scientific inquiry. One important person who did this was a Franciscan friar named Roger Bacon. He advanced the scientific method inspired by Aristotle. As a result, European scholars, like their Greek predecessors, began relying more on formulating hypotheses and theories based on careful observation and less on mythology, religion, and the supernatural to improve their understanding of the natural world, even as church officials punished them for this so-called heretical behavior.

The SCIENTIFIC REVOLUTION: COPERNICUS and GALILEO

In 1543, a Polish mathematician and astronomer named Nicolaus Copernicus (1473–1543) shared the first significant discovery of the Scientific Revolution when he published a

The Copernican model of the solar system places the sun, rather than Earth, at the center.

book called *On the Revolutions of the Heavenly Spheres*. The contents of this book mathematically proved the heliocentric nature of the solar system. Copernicus most likely made this discovery independently of the ancient Greeks, who had formulated (though not proven) a similar model. (Incidentally this was just one example of the early use of mathematics as the "language" of nature.) Later, church officials would deem the Copernican model of the solar system "foolish and absurd in philosophy, and formally heretical since it explicitly contradicts in many places the sense of Holy Scripture."

Italian scientist Galileo Galilei revolutionized our understanding of the laws of motion.

Another key figure of the Scientific Revolution was an Italian scholar named Galileo Galilei (1564–1642). Galileo performed mechanical experiments that revolutionized our understanding of the laws of motion. For example, it was Galileo who determined that all bodies accelerate at the same rate regardless of size or mass. Galileo also developed the conceptualization of motion in terms of speed and direction (velocity), recognized force as a cause for motion, and observed that objects in motion resist change (inertia).

Despite the church's declaration that the Copernican model of the solar system was heretical, Galileo spoke out in support of it. Church officials quickly arrested and tried Galileo. They found him "vehemently suspect of heresy"; ordered him to "to abstain completely from teaching or defending this doctrine and opinion or from discussing it," "to abandon completely … the opinion that the sun stands still at the center of the world and the earth moves," and "henceforth not to hold, teach, or defend it in any way whatever, either orally or in writing"; and placed him under house arrest for the rest of his life. This unfortunate turn of events did little to diminish Galileo's considerable reputation, however. Indeed, according to physicist Stephen Hawking (1942–2018), "Galileo, perhaps more than any other single person, was responsible for the birth of modern science."

SIR ISAAC NEWTON

The scientific community found a more-than-worthy successor to Galileo in Sir Isaac Newton (1642–1727). In 1687, Newton published an important work called the

Sir Isaac Newton's theories remained the prevailing scientific paradigm for more than two hundred years.

Mathematica Principles of Natural Philosophy, often referred to as the *Principia*. It was the culmination of years of study.

The *Principia* outlined three laws of motion. The first stated that a body at rest will remain at rest (unless an outside force acts on it) and that a body in motion at a constant velocity will remain in motion in a straight line (again, unless an outside force acts on it).

The second stated that if an outside force acts on a body, that body will experience a change of speed. The third stated that for every action, there is an equal and opposite reaction. Together, these three laws, which described a world as predictable as a mechanical clock in which identical conditions produced identical results, laid the foundation for the field of physics.

The *Principia* also presented Newton's law of universal gravitation. This law stated that every mass, or particle of matter, exerts an attractive force (gravity) on every other mass. It also laid down the mathematical formula to describe this force.

But this law didn't simply recognize and mathematically define gravity. It also posited that gravity existed not just on Earth but everywhere in the universe.

At first Newton's theories faced tremendous opposition. But after a time, this opposition evaporated. Indeed, the Newtonian model of physics—not just its laws and principles, but its predictability—remained the prevailing scientific paradigm for more than two hundred years and was the platform upon which all subsequent developments rested.

The LIMITATIONS of NEWTONIAN PHYSICS

By the turn of the twentieth century, most learned people believed Newtonian physics accurately described the inner workings of the universe. In other words, the universe was rather like a mechanical clock: entirely predictable. All that was left, they believed, was to improve methodologies and seek more accurate methods of measurement.

At the turn of the twentieth century, however, something new was discovered in physics. This occurred after scientists noticed certain natural phenomena that could not be described by Newtonian physics. One such phenomenon was called the blackbody radiation problem. A blackbody is a theoretical "perfect" surface. Scientists hypothesized (and experiments seemed to support) that while in a state of equilibrium, a blackbody both absorbed and emitted all frequencies, or wavelengths, of nearby thermal radiation— from gamma rays to ultraviolet rays to visible light to infrared light to microwaves to radio waves to ultra-low frequency waves and beyond.

While attempting to prove this hypothesis mathematically, two British scientists, Lord Rayleigh (1842–1919) and Sir James Jeans (1877–1946) discovered that the intensity of the thermal radiation emitted depended on the radiation's frequency and wavelength and on the temperature of the blackbody itself—unless the frequency was in the ultraviolet range or higher, with very short wavelengths, in which case it became chaotic and disordered. (Scientists referred to this phenomenon as the ultraviolet catastrophe.)

Another scientist, named Wilhelm Wien (1864–1928), took another approach. He was similarly unsuccessful. Only in his case, things fell apart when the frequency hit the infrared range or lower, with very long wavelengths. This was strange. Scientists had long understood that all normal matter emitted radiation. Presumably they would be able to apply basic physics to explain this. But when it came to explaining blackbody radiation, applying basic physics just didn't work.

In December 1900, a German mathematician named Max Planck hit on an explanation for the blackbody radiation problem. Planck posited that the radiation emitted by a heated object was the result of energy emitted by atoms vibrating inside the object. As Planck attempted to compose an equation to prove this hypothesis, he grew increasingly frustrated.

Finally, he concluded that the math would be simpler if he assumed that the amount of energy in these atoms was restricted to values of a certain range rather than given some arbitrary value. Planck—in what he called "an act of desperation"—decided to first solve the equation using these ranges, or increments, and figure out how to adjust it to accommodate all values later on. The problem was, Planck's equation couldn't accommodate all values. It could only accommodate the incremental ones.

At first, Planck had no idea why his equation worked the way it did. Eventually, he came to understand that the fact that his equation could accommodate incremental values but not all values indicated that the energy emitted by the vibrating atoms in blackbody radiation was quantized rather than continuous. This idea of quantized energy means that rather than being emitted in a gradual manner, this energy—indeed, all energy—was emitted in tiny and instantaneous bursts. From this, scientists concluded that energy existed only in unified bundles, called quanta (the singular form of quantum, from the Latin *quantus*, meaning "how many"), and had characteristics that were quite different from the prevailing paradigm.

Another phenomenon that could not be explained by Newtonian physics was the photoelectric effect. The photoelectric effect occurs when ultraviolet radiation falls on a metal surface. Electrons inside the metal either flow along

Max Planck is considered the father of quantum physics.

its surface or are ejected from the material. (An electron is a kind of particle found inside an atom.)

Scientific calculations indicated that it should take several seconds for sufficient energy to accumulate at any individual atom to eject an electron. Experience, however, showed something different: the instant the ultraviolet radiation struck the metal surface, atoms started ejecting electrons.

In 1905, armed with Planck's conclusions, a German scientist named Albert Einstein solved this mystery. He supposed that the bursts of energy described by Planck created tiny "lumps" of radiation, or light, that traveled through space. (Today we call these lumps of light photons.) Einstein correctly posited that a single photon could deliver all its energy to a single atom on the metal surface.

This concentrated energy, assuming it was adequately strong, could instantly eject an electron. "According to the assumption to be contemplated here," Einstein wrote, "when a light ray is spreading from a point, the energy is not distributed continuously over ever-increasing spaces, but consists of a finite number of 'energy quanta' that are localized in points in space, move without dividing, and can be absorbed or generated only as a whole." Einstein biographer Albrecht Fölsing called this "the most 'revolutionary' sentence written by a physicist of the twentieth century."

The notion that atoms contained particles (like electrons) that acted as discrete packets of energy—and, later, the discovery that these packets of energy had wave-like properties (discussed in chapter 4)—formed the foundation of a new and important field of scientific study called quantum physics. Physicist Leon Lederman describes this discovery as "the most seminal change in viewpoint since the early Greeks gave up mythology to initiate the search for a rational understanding of the universe."

In the years to come, scientists would look to quantum physics (sometimes called quantum mechanics), and to Einstein's theories of relativity (which, incidentally, do not take quantum physics into account), to describe the inner workings of our universe.

But they did not discard classical, or Newtonian, physics. Many classical principles remain quite valid—at least for objects that are larger than an atom or molecule all the way up to objects the size of our universe. It's not that the rules of quantum physics do not apply to larger objects. It's that, for larger objects, classical physics provides an excellent approximation of these quantum rules. It is for this reason that classical physics remains the foundation for most modern engineering fields.

Einstein's Theories of Relativity

Albert Einstein made important contributions to quantum physics, but he is most famous for his development of the theories of special and general relativity and for the formulation of the equation $E = mc^2$. This equation basically means that the mass (m) of a body times the speed of light (c^2) is equal to the kinetic energy (E) of that body.

The theory of special relativity proposes that simultaneity is relative—that is, two events that appear simultaneous from one point of reference might not seem simultaneous from another. For example, imagine you're riding in the middle car in a long train moving at a constant speed. Suddenly two bolts of lightning strike the train—one at the front and one at the back. Because you are riding in the middle of the train, these strikes seem simultaneous. But if you were riding in the front or the back, you would perceive the bolt that struck there first. Therefore, Einstein concluded, time itself is relative. Einstein's theory of special relativity also asserts that nothing can travel faster than the speed of light.

The theory of general relativity is concerned with gravity. It describes the behavior of objects on the universal scale, such as stars, planets, and black holes, and the evolution of the universe as a whole. With these theories, Einstein refined our understanding of fundamental concepts like space, time, matter, energy, and gravity. Interestingly, Einstein's theories of relativity do not account for the existence of quantum physics. Scientists are working to develop a theory of everything that unifies both.

Special relativity has passed numerous tests for over one hundred years. However, scientists in Switzerland have recently found that when they beamed neutrinos 454 miles (730 kilometers) underground to Italy and calculated the speed, the neutrinos seemed to beat the speed of light by sixty billionths of a second. Special relativity postulates that if something does indeed travel faster than the speed of light, then it actually travels backward in time. This finding has enormous implications for a proposition called causality—the idea that cause comes before effect. Put another way, the experiment raises the question of whether time travel would be possible.

X-rays are electromagnetic waves of high energy and short wavelengths carried by photons. They have been essential in quantum mechanics research.

CHAPTER 2

The Science of Quantum Mechanics

I n solving the problem of blackbody radiation, Max Planck discovered that atoms did not emit energy in a continuous manner. Rather, bundles of energy, called quanta, were released in tiny and instantaneous bursts. The same cannot be said of the process of scientific discovery, however. These discoveries rarely occur instantaneously. Rather, they are usually the result of a continuous and long-lasting effort by one or more scientists to identify and seek solutions to specific scientific problems. These efforts rarely involve a linear progression. Sometimes scientists take wrong turns. Other times scientists solve the problem, only to discover a new one.

Such was the case for the problems of both blackbody radiation and the photoelectric effect. Before scientists could identify—let alone solve—these problems, they needed a solid understanding of the structure and behavior of atoms; the nature of light; the workings of electricity; the nature of fields (or, more precisely, of energy); thermodynamics;

electromagnetic radiation; and more. Developing this understanding took time.

The SCIENTIFIC METHOD

In order to study and understand the many questions in the field of quantum mechanics, scientists need some sort of foundation to examine their theories and observations. Scientists use a specific methodology to draw conclusions about the world around them. This method is called the scientific method, and it remains in use today.

The steps of the modern scientific method include making observations; developing questions about the observations; formulating a hypothesis about the observations; developing predictions; gathering data (through experimentation and/or the application of mathematics) to test the predictions; refining, altering, expanding, or rejecting the hypothesis; developing a general theory; and beginning the cycle anew. By employing the scientific method, scientists increase the rigor of scientific inquiry as well as the likelihood that the general theories they develop are correct.

The scientific method reflects a key tenet of scientific study: scientific ideas are not set in stone. They are considered to be true only to the extent that they are verifiable through rational thought, experimentation, and mathematics. And the possibility always remains that new rational thought, experimentation, and mathematics could disprove them.

The STUDY of ATOMS

One early step toward the discovery of quantum physics was the identification of the atom. The ancient Greeks conceived of an atom-like structure sometime around 400 BCE, called an *a-tomo* (Greek for "not able to be cut" or "without parts"). An a-tomo represented the smallest possible particle of a given piece of matter.

More than two thousand years later, Sir Isaac Newton took an interest in the fundamental composition of matter. He proposed that matter was made of "solid, massy, hard, impenetrable, moveable particles" formed by God. "These primitive particles being solids," he explained, "are incomparably harder than any porous bodies compounded of them; even so very hard as never to wear or break in pieces: no ordinary power being able to divide what God himself made one in the first Creation." Ultimately, these particles, which Newton called corpuscles, were not unlike the a-tomos envisioned by the early Greeks. However, unlike a-tomos, corpuscles could conceivably be divided into even smaller particles and still retain all their characteristics and could attract other similar particles at close range. Newton's corpuscle is widely viewed as the predecessor of the atom.

In 1714, a German scientist named Gottfried Leibniz (1646–1716) developed an alternative model for the atom, which he called a monad. He described monads as "the elements out of which everything is made" and believed "every monad is a mirror of the universe in its own way." Apart from asserting that each monad was a tiny point of energy and contained no smaller parts, Leibniz declined to describe the physical structure of the nomad in detail. He did describe its qualities, however. One characteristic of the monad was its unification in nature, meaning the only way for a monad to come into or go out of existence was instantaneously. He described this as "being created or annihilated all at once." Another characteristic was that each monad was "qualitatively unlike every other." Finally, a third characteristic was that monads underwent constant change, both structural and behavioral, and that this change could result only from the application of internal (rather than external) forces.

During the mid-1700s, a Croatian mathematician named Ruđer Bošković (1711–1787) combined Newton's sense of corpuscles as elementary particles that could attract at close distances with Leibniz's view of monads as points of energy to create a new atomic theory. Bošković believed atoms were simply points (called "atom points") surrounded by fields with positive and negative charges that could both attract (at short distances) and repel (from farther away) other atom points. Atom points could combine to form both chemical elements and compounds made of these elements. The chemical composition of these elements and compounds resulted from the pattern of the fields surrounding the atom points.

Despite these earlier advancements, history credits a British scientist named John Dalton (1766–1844) with the identification of the atom. After years of research, Dalton concluded in 1803 that all matter was made of microscopic particles called atoms and that atoms were both indivisible and indestructible. Dalton also determined that all atoms of a given chemical element—such as hydrogen, oxygen, nitrogen, and so forth—were identical in mass and properties. In other words, each chemical element had its own unique type of atom. Dalton then deduced that compounds were formed by a combination of two or more different kinds of atoms. (We call these molecules.) Finally, Dalton ascertained that a chemical reaction is in fact a rearrangement of atoms.

Generally speaking, Dalton's atomic model has stood the test of time, but it doesn't tell the whole story. Further research into atoms revealed that they were not the smallest possible particles of matter. Indeed, as scientists would later discover, atoms themselves contained even smaller masses, and these tiny masses dictated the behavior of matter on a grand scale.

The NATURE of LIGHT

Just as Dalton concluded matter was made of small particles (called atoms), many scientists, including Newton, had long believed light rays were particulate in nature. Others, however, posed a different theory: that light rays were in fact emitted in wave form.

In 1801, a British scientist named Thomas Young (1773–1829) attempted to settle this matter. He conducted a simple experiment that involved projecting light rays from a single concentrated source through two thin slits onto a screen. As the light passed through the slits it created an interference pattern on the screen, indicating that the light traveled in waves rather than particles. However, the interference pattern itself was composed of tiny points on the screen, suggesting that even as it traveled in waves, light acted like particles. This phenomenon came to be called wave-particle duality.

Even after Young published his findings, many of his contemporaries remained unconvinced. Further experiments by Augustin-Jean Fresnel (1788–1827) in 1818 confirmed Young was correct, at least to a certain extent. Studies in quantum physics would later reveal things were in fact a little more complicated.

The STUDY of ELECTRICITY

Even in ancient times, people had some awareness of the existence of electricity—primarily through contact with electric fish, such as the electric eel, which produced a powerful jolt. They also had some experience with static electricity, having noticed that rubbing amber on fur could attract certain lightweight objects such as feathers. On a related note, by the 1400s, the Arabs had surmised that lightning had electrical properties, and they even had a word for it: *ra'ad*. But it wasn't until the late 1500s that electricity became a serious subject of scientific inquiry in the Western world.

A British scientist named William Gilbert (1544–1603) was among the first to differentiate electricity (which produced the interaction between amber and fur) from magnetism (evident when one object was naturally drawn to another). However, later scientists would conclude that both were in fact the product of a single force called electromagnetism. Gilbert also coined a new Latin term, *electricus* (from *elektron*, the Greek word for "amber"), to describe this phenomenon.

During the late 1500s, electricity became a topic of serious scientific study.

An American autodidact named Benjamin Franklin (1706–1790) observed that electricity involved two types of charges: positive and negative. Objects with a positive charge attracted objects with a negative charge (and vice versa). However, two objects with the same charge—positive or negative—repelled each other. (In a famous experiment that involved flying a kite during a thunderstorm, Franklin also determined that lightning was indeed electric.)

During the 1800s, scientists developed an excellent grasp on how electricity worked. For example, they discovered that electrical charges can move, and when they do, they are said to create a current. (When a current followed a particular path, that path was called a circuit.) They also identified substances through which current could flow, which they called conductors. This ushered in an era of tremendous innovation and invention, including the electric battery, telegraph, telephone, lightbulb, and other important technologies. However, it would be some time before scientists understood why electricity worked.

The DISCOVERY of FIELDS

Newtonian physics seemed to suggest that the universe consisted of atoms moving through empty space and interacting only through direct contact or direct action. However, a self-taught scientist named Michael Faraday (1791–1867) perceived one key weakness in this model. He noticed that it failed to account for the behavior of magnets, which could pull iron—and could push or pull other magnets—without direct contact or action.

Faraday determined that the presence of a magnet altered the space around it, and this alteration, which Faraday called a magnetic field, was a characteristic, or property, of space itself. In other words, Faraday proved that space was not nothing. It wasn't empty. It didn't simply serve as a location in which objects existed. Faraday also concluded that forces like magnetism and electricity existed not in objects but in space itself. This discovery represents the birth of a new branch of science called field theory.

This and other breakthroughs by Faraday—such as his identification of one of the basic laws of electromagnetism, called electromagnetic induction, which describes how magnetic fields interact with an electric circuit, and his understanding of the underlying relationship between magnetism and light—proved revolutionary.

Faraday was extremely intelligent, but his mathematical skills were limited. In 1865, a physicist named James Clerk Maxwell published a treatise called *A Dynamical Theory of the Electromagnetic Field*. This summarized the work of Faraday and others into a comprehensive set of differential equations that described the behavior of electromagnetic fields and served as the foundation for all modern theories pertaining to electromagnetism. It also predicted the existence of electromagnetic waves that moved at or near the speed of light. Moreover, it identified visible light rays, as well as invisible rays such as infrared (discovered in 1800) and ultraviolet (identified in 1801) as types of electromagnetic waves.

Albert Einstein would rely heavily on the work of Faraday and Maxwell in his own research. Indeed, Einstein hung photos of both men, along with a painted image of Sir Isaac Newton, in his study. "Before Maxwell, Physical Reality ... was thought of as consisting in material particles," Einstein wrote. "Since Maxwell's time, Physical Reality has been thought of as represented by continuous fields." Einstein concluded, "This change in the conception of Reality is the most profound and the most fruitful that physics has experienced since the time of Newton."

The STUDY of THERMODYNAMICS

As noted in chapter 1, the blackbody radiation problem, solved by Max Planck, pertained to the emission of thermal radiation from a theoretical physical body. Thermodynamics is the branch of physics concerned with such matters. More precisely, thermodynamics deals with the relationships between all forms of energy, including heat, mechanical energy, electrical energy, chemical energy, and so forth.

In the 1600s, scientists correctly concluded that heat was related to the motion of atoms inside matter. A famous British scientist named Francis Bacon (1561–1626) described it as follows: "Heat itself, its essence and quiddity, is motion and nothing else." (Quiddity is defined as the inherent nature of something.) Scientists rejected this view during the 1700s, concluding instead that heat was in fact a massless and fluid-like substance, called caloric. However, further experimentation during the 1800s proved its veracity.

The invention of the steam engine in 1712 revealed the relationship between heat and work. (In this context "work" describes the transfer of energy from one place or form to another.) In essence, these engines consisted of a heating element (such as burning coal), a reservoir filled with water, and one or more cylinders containing a tightly fitted piston. One end of each piston connected to the machine that the engine was meant to power. The engine operated by heating the water in the reservoir to a boil. As the boiling water turned into steam, the pressure inside the reservoir rose, causing the piston inside each cylinder to move up and down. This up-and-down movement drove the mechanism of the attached machine.

Scientists had an intuitive understanding of how these engines operated. What they lacked was a scientific theory to explain it. Research by a series of scientists throughout the 1800s revealed the answer, referred to as the mechanical theory of heat. This theory, as articulated by Lord Kelvin, claimed that heat was "a dynamical form of mechanical effect." He continued: "We perceive that there must be an equivalence between mechanical work and heat, as between cause and effect." In other words, mechanical work and heat were essentially interchangeable, and both were forms of energy. Moreover, just as heat caused mechanical work (as with a steam engine), mechanical work caused heat (for example, through friction).

During the 1840s, a British physicist named James Prescott Joule (1818–1889) quantified the relationship between work and heat. Through experimentation, Joule identified the mechanical equivalent of heat—that is, how much work (generated by friction) it took to heat a given amount of water to a specified temperature. In addition to pinpointing this numeric value (now called a "joule"), Joule also determined that a given amount of work would always generate the same amount of heat, no matter what.

Michael Faraday

Michael Faraday was born in 1791, in a small village near London. He was one of four children in a family of meager means. Although he received only the most rudimentary education, Faraday became interested in science at a young age.

One day Faraday obtained a ticket to attend a series of lectures by a celebrated chemist named Sir Humphry Davy. During each lecture, Faraday scribbled copious notes. Afterward, he sent them to Davy—along with a query regarding employment. Davy hired Faraday as his laboratory assistant.

By 1820, Faraday had become an expert in chemistry. He soon began developing his own areas of research. Faraday's early research led to the discovery of several chemical compounds. Later, Faraday switched to studying electricity and magnetism.

In 1821, Faraday married Sarah Barnard, whom he met at church. The couple—who shared a deep Christian faith—enjoyed a happy marriage, but they had no children. Sadly, Faraday suffered a nervous breakdown in 1839. He returned to work in 1845, and he enjoyed a decade of productivity. After that, Faraday's mind grew feeble, and he died in 1867.

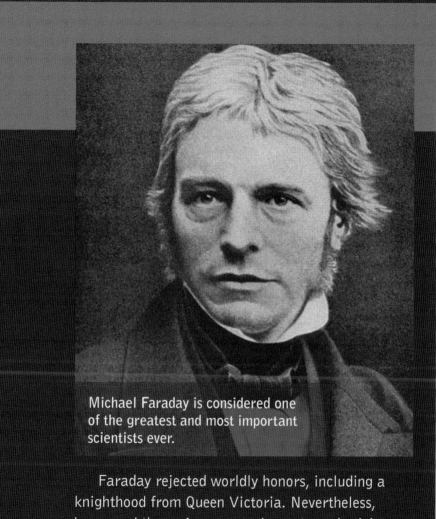

Michael Faraday is considered one of the greatest and most important scientists ever.

Faraday rejected worldly honors, including a knighthood from Queen Victoria. Nevertheless, he earned them. As renowned quantum physicist Ernest Rutherford (1871–1937) put it, "When we consider the magnitude and extent of his discoveries and their influence on the progress of science and of industry, there is no honour too great to pay to the memory of Faraday, one of the greatest scientific discoverers of all time."

Ultimately, scientists concluded that it wasn't just that work and heat were interchangeable. It was that all forms of energy were. As observed by German chemist Karl Friedrich Mohr (1806–1879), energy "can under suitable conditions appear as motion, cohesion, electricity, light, heat, and magnetism." This notion had powerful implications and served as the basis of the first law of thermodynamics. This law—definitively stated in 1847 and often called the law of conservation of energy—asserts that energy in a closed system can be neither created nor destroyed (although it can change form). A second law of thermodynamics, formally stated in 1874, asserted that entropy—which describes the heat lost or wasted (having been converted to some other form of energy) during some type of process—increases over time. These and other principles of thermodynamics would factor heavily into the study of quantum physics.

The DISCOVERY of ELECTROMAGNETIC RADIATION

In 1865, James Clerk Maxwell hypothesized the existence of electromagnetic waves that moved at or near the speed of light (and that light itself—along with infrared rays and ultraviolet rays—was one such type of electromagnetic wave). Maxwell never confirmed this hypothesis through experimentation, however. That task fell to a German physicist named Heinrich Hertz (1857–1894). In 1888, Hertz developed an apparatus that both transmitted and received low-frequency electromagnetic waves (later called radio waves) through the air. These invisible waves behaved

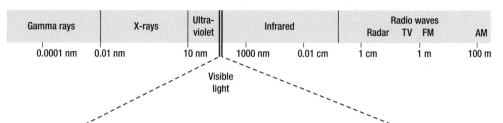

| Gamma rays | X-rays | Ultra-violet | Infrared | Radio waves |
| | | | | Radar TV FM | AM |

0.0001 nm   0.01 nm   10 nm   1000 nm   0.01 cm   1 cm   1 m   100 m

Visible
light

VISIBLE SPECTRUM

The visible spectrum is just a small part of the electromagnetic spectrum.

just like light—subject to such properties as reflection, refraction, diffraction, and interference.

After his discovery of radio waves, someone asked Hertz about the applications of his discovery. His answer: "Nothing, I guess." In his mind, the sole significance of his discovery was that it proved "Maestro Maxwell was right." In this assessment, however, Hertz was quite wrong. His discovery of radio waves would lead to the invention of the radio, the television, radar, electromagnetic imaging, wireless communications, and more.

In addition, discoveries of more types of electromagnetic waves soon followed, such as microwaves, X-rays, gamma rays, and others. Today, scientists organize all these types of electromagnetic waves into an electromagnetic spectrum, from the highest frequency and shortest waves (gamma rays) to the lowest frequency and longest waves (extremely low frequency waves). (Note that sound waves are not electromagnetic waves. Rather, they are the result of an oscillating compression of molecules. Hence, they do not fall on the spectrum.) It's no wonder scientists named the unit of frequency—cycles per second—the "hertz"!

The IDENTIFICATION of the ELECTRON

As mentioned, during the 1800s, scientists developed a comprehensive understanding of what electricity did and how it behaved. What they didn't understand was what an electrical current was made of.

Scientists were particularly confused by the behavior of a type of energy called cathode rays. This behavior could be observed when scientists applied voltage to two electrodes

J. J. Thomson discovered the electron.

on either end of a vacuum tube. One electrode connected to the positive terminal of the voltage supply. This electrode was called an anode.

The other electrode, called the cathode, connected to the voltage supply's negative terminal. When the voltage was applied, a visible ray of energy, called a cathode ray, streamed from the cathode end of the tube to the anode end.

Scientists had no idea what these rays were made of. Indeed, observed British scientist J. J. Thomson (1856–1940), "The most diverse opinions [were] held as to these rays." In a paper on the subject, Thomson, a physics professor at Cambridge University, observed that "according to the almost unanimous opinion of German physicists they are due to some process in the aether to which … no phenomenon hitherto observed is analogous." Another view was that they were in fact "wholly material, and that they mark the paths of particles of matter charged with negative electricity."

Through extensive experimentation, Thomson ultimately concluded that the scientists who held that cathode rays marked the paths of negatively charged particles were indeed correct.

But Thomson took this view one step further, positing that the particles were in fact something he called "primordial atoms" and that the atoms comprising chemical elements were "an aggregation of a number of primordial atoms."

In other words, these primordial atoms—which Thomson ascertained to be identical to each other and infinitesimal in size—were subatomic particles existing inside an atom. Thomson then asserted that these primordial atoms represented "matter in a new state, a state in which the subdivision of matter is carried very much further than [before]." Moreover, he claimed, this matter was "the substance from which all the chemical elements are built up." This was a shocking claim. Hitherto, most scientists believed atoms to be indivisible and, as such, the most basic unit of matter.

Later, scientists called Thomson's primordial atoms "electrons." They also discovered other types of subatomic particles, including protons, neutrons, quarks, leptons, bosons, and more. In the next chapter, we will learn about the important scientists who contributed to our understanding of quantum mechanics.

As a field of study, quantum mechanics is comprised of the knowledge from the discoveries of many scientists. From those who studied atoms to those who discovered electromagnetism, quantum mechanics research is built upon the contributions of scientists and philosophers throughout history. It is even more impressive that these figures were conducting experiments all around the world. But, they still managed to collaborate and even form lasting friendships.

Max Planck (*left*) and Albert Einstein (*right*) had a strong relationship as friends and colleagues.

CHAPTER 3

The Fathers of Quantum Mechanics

Many physicists contributed to the early development of quantum physics. This chapter introduces several of these scientists: Max Planck, Albert Einstein, Niels Bohr, Louis de Broglie, Max Born, Erwin Schrödinger, Wolfgang Pauli, Werner Heisenberg, and Paul Dirac. These physicists had much in common. Planck, Einstein, Born, Schrödinger, Pauli, and Heisenberg shared a Germanic or Austrian heritage. Planck, Einstein, and Heisenberg were musically inclined. Planck, Einstein, and Heisenberg were religious, but Born, Bohr, de Broglie, Schrödinger, Pauli, and Dirac were avowed atheists. (Dirac described religion as "a kind of opium that allows a nation to lull itself into wishful dreams and so forget the injustices that are being perpetrated against the people.") Several of these scientists attended or taught at the same universities and collaborated in research, and many of them became great friends. All of them won a Nobel Prize in Physics. The achievements of these scientists, and their contributions to quantum physics, cannot be overstated.

MAX PLANCK (1858–1947)

Max Planck discovered that a theoretical blackbody emitted energy in short bursts rather than continuously. His work also helped scientists understand atomic and subatomic processes. These scientific contributions spurred the development of quantum physics.

Planck was born in Kiel, which later became part of the German Empire, on April 23, 1858. Later, Planck's family—father Julius, mother Emma, five siblings, and two half siblings—moved to Munich, where Julius worked as a university professor.

Planck was a gifted musician and a gifted physicist. After careful consideration, Planck chose to pursue physics at the University of Munich despite being told by his physics professor that "almost everything is already discovered, and all that remains is to fill a few holes."

Planck earned his doctorate degree in 1879. After that he worked at the University of Kiel and, later, at the University of Berlin. Planck's early research centered on thermodynamics. Later he focused on understanding the ramifications of quantum physics. Planck was awarded several academic prizes, including the Nobel Prize in Physics (1918). One student described Planck as the best lecturer he had ever heard.

In 1887, Planck married Marie Merck. The couple enjoyed a happy marriage and had four children: Karl, twins Emma and Grete, and Erwin. Marie died of tuberculosis in 1909. Over the next decade, three of Planck's children also died: Karl (1916), who was killed during the Great War

(World War I), and Grete (1917) and Emma (1919), who both died during childbirth. In 1911, Planck married Marie's cousin, Marga von Hösslin, who bore one son, Hermann.

Germany's defeat in the Great War left the country destitute. Funding for research dried up. In 1933, the Nazi Party gained power. The Nazis expelled and humiliated many of Planck's Jewish friends and colleagues. Then, the Nazis trained their crosshairs on Planck himself for teaching theories developed by Jewish scientists. They did not arrest Planck, who was Lutheran, but they did force him to step down from his various academic posts.

World War II proved particularly painful for Planck. In 1944, Allied bombs obliterated his home in Berlin (and with it all his notes and correspondence). In 1945, Gestapo agents brutally murdered his son Erwin for his role in a plot to assassinate Hitler. This last loss left Planck a broken man. He died on October 4, 1947. He was eighty-nine years old.

ALBERT EINSTEIN (1885–1962)

Albert Einstein confirmed the quantum nature of energy by solving the problem of the photoelectric effect and conceived the notion of the photon. But he is most famous for articulating theories relating to relativity and his formulation of the equation $E = mc^2$.

Einstein was born on March 14, 1879, in the German city of Ulm. He had one younger sister. His parents were Hermann and Pauline. In 1880, Hermann moved the family to Munich and started a business manufacturing electrical equipment.

Einstein showed an early aptitude for music, but little else revealed his incredible intellect. He was also notoriously difficult in school. Einstein did earn a degree in science and mathematics, but his professors had found him so frustrating that they refused to help him obtain a job in academia.

Einstein eventually accepted a post at the Swiss patent office, but he continued his research in science and mathematics. In 1905, he published four ground-breaking papers. Afterward he was able to find work in an academic setting, holding a series of posts at various academic institutions. In 1921, Einstein won the Nobel Prize in Physics.

Einstein married a classmate named Mileva Marić in 1903. They had two sons. The couple divorced in 1919, and Einstein married a woman named Elsa Löwenthal. Einstein adopted Elsa's two daughters from a previous marriage. Elsa died in 1936.

The ascent of the Nazi regime derailed Einstein's career. Because Einstein was Jewish, he was barred from holding a university position in Germany. In 1933, Einstein immigrated to America and accepted a position at Princeton University. He remained there for the remainder of his career.

As his career progressed, Einstein grew increasingly disenchanted with quantum physics. "Quantum mechanics is very impressive," he wrote a friend. "But an inner voice tells me that it is not yet the real thing." Ultimately, says science writer Katie Silver, Einstein "wanted to create a theory that would bring together gravity and the rest of physics, with all the quantum weirdness as a secondary consequence." During the last thirty years of his career, Einstein worked tirelessly to piece together such a theory. In this endeavor he was unsuccessful.

On April 16, 1955, Einstein experienced an abdominal aortic aneurysm. He died the next day at the age of seventy-six.

NIELS BOHR (1885–1962)

Niels Bohr applied the principles of quantum physics to the atom to develop a new model to describe its structure. Bohr also studied radioactivity and predicted the existence of various chemical elements.

Bohr was born on October 7, 1885, in Copenhagen, Denmark. His father, Christian, was a university professor. His mother, Ellen, came from a family of prominent Jewish bankers. Bohr had an older sister and a younger brother. As a child, Bohr was a talented football (soccer) player, but he quickly grasped that his future lay in academia.

Bohr commenced his studies at the University of Copenhagen in 1903. He focused on physics, astronomy, mathematics, and philosophy. He earned his master's degree in 1909 and a doctorate degree in 1911.

After holding academic posts at various institutions, Bohr returned to the University of Copenhagen in 1916. There, in addition to serving as chair of Theoretical Physics, he founded the Institute of Theoretical Physics. In 1922, Bohr won the Nobel Prize in Physics for his work investigating the structure of atoms and the radiation that emanates from them.

In 1910, Bohr met Margrethe Nørlund. The couple married two years later. The daughter of a pharmacist, Margrethe was instrumental to Bohr's success. As one family friend observed, she had "a decisive role in making his whole scientific and personal activity possible and harmonious. One of the couple's six children (all sons) agreed, noting that "her opinions were his guidelines in daily affairs."

Although Bohr was not German, the Nazis disrupted his career. In 1940, the Nazis occupied Denmark. Three years later, they determined that due to his mother's heritage, Bohr was Jewish. Assisted by the Danish resistance, Bohr and his family escaped first to Sweden and then to England. The British tapped Bohr to join several British scientists involved in the Manhattan Project (the name given to the American nuclear weapons research program). In this capacity, recalled physicist Robert Oppenheimer (1904–1967), who led the project, Bohr acted "as a scientific father figure to the younger men." After the war, Bohr became a powerful advocate for international cooperation with regard to nuclear energy.

On November 18, 1962, Bohr died of heart failure in his Copenhagen home. He was seventy-seven years old.

LOUIS DE BROGLIE (1892–1987)

Louis de Broglie predicted the wave-like behavior of particles such as electrons and hypothesized that all matter has wave properties.

The youngest of five children, de Broglie was born on August 15, 1892, in Dieppe, France. His father, Victor, was a French duke. De Broglie earned a degree in history at the Sorbonne in 1909. Afterward, he decided to study physics. De Broglie was particularly intrigued by the conceptual side of physics. He had, he said, "much more the state of

Louis de Broglie predicted the wave-like behavior of particles such as electrons and hypothesized that all matter has wave properties.

The Institute of Theoretical Physics

In 1921, Niels Bohr founded the Institute of Theoretical Physics at the University of Copenhagen, one of the most influential centers of thought on quantum physics in the world. In a letter sent in 1923, Bohr outlined his vision for the institute:

> I wish very much to be able to receive as many properly qualified physicists as possible and to offer them good working conditions, so that they may be able to carry on with the greatest possible vigor the development of atomic physics which has given and continually promises most important results, and so that by the training of foreign physicists it may be possible to cooperate with physical and chemical institutes and unite them in their work.

Bohr fulfilled this vision. According to the Nobel Group, "Niels Bohr created a fundamental change in thinking in physics and at the same time he managed to create an international environment that attracted some of the best scientists from around the world." These included luminaries such

The Niels Bohr Institute is located at the University of Copenhagen in Denmark.

as Werner Heisenberg, Paul Dirac, Wolfgang Pauli, and many others.

During the growing Nazi threat of the 1930s and 1940s, the institute provided a safe haven for Jewish scientists and other scientists targeted by the Third Reich. In addition to offering these scientists temporary employment, Bohr supported them financially, arranged for them to receive fellowships, and helped them find permanent positions at academic institutions all over the world.

Nearly one hundred years after its founding, the institute—now called the Niels Bohr Institute—continues to thrive.

mind of a pure theoretician than that of an experimenter or engineer" and especially loved "the general and philosophical view."

In 1914, the Great War briefly put the brakes on de Broglie's studies. He enlisted in the army and served with French engineers at a wireless radio station under the Eiffel Tower. After the war, de Broglie returned to the Sorbonne, where he earned his doctorate degree in physics in 1924. His doctoral thesis—inspired by work done by Max Planck and Albert Einstein on the nature of light—outlined his hypothesis regarding the wave-like behavior of particles. To de Broglie's delight, Einstein himself was extremely impressed with the thesis.

In 1928, the university granted de Broglie a professorship. He remained in that post until his retirement in 1962. But de Broglie's reach was wider than just the Sorbonne. He also served in the Académie Française (which acts as the official authority on the French language) as well as in the Académie des Sciences (which encourages scientific research in France).

World War II proved less disruptive to de Broglie's career than to that of his German colleagues. He remained at the Sorbonne for the duration of the war. Afterward, he served as an advisor to the French High Commission of Atomic Energy.

Over the course of his career, de Broglie published more than twenty books and dozens of research papers on a variety of scientific topics. His personal life was perhaps less prolific. De Broglie, who never married, enjoyed a withdrawn existence. Upon the death of his older brother in 1960, de Broglie inherited the title of duke.

De Broglie died of natural causes on March 19, 1987, in Louveciennes, France. He was ninety-four years old.

MAX BORN (1882–1970)

Max Born is best known for his work on the wave function, which describes the wave characteristics of a particle in mathematical terms.

Born was born into an upper-middle-class Jewish family on December 11, 1882, in the German city of Breslau (now part of Poland). Born's father, Gustav, was a university professor. Sadly, Born's mother, Gretchen, died when Born was four years old. Born had one sister and one half brother.

At university, Born studied physics and mathematics. He earned his doctorate degree in 1907. Afterward he conducted postdoctorate research on Einstein's theory of special relativity.

In 1913, Born married Hedwig Ehrenberg. They had three children. Although the marriage was an unhappy one, it lasted for fifty-seven years. In 1915, Born was drafted into the German army to serve during the Great War. Born worked first as a radio operator and later in a research position where he studied sound ranging (a way to identify the enemy's coordinates based on sound). After the war, Born accepted a position at the University of Frankfurt. Two years later, in 1921, he switched to the University of Göttingen. There he built one of the most important and respected physics programs in Europe.

Like Einstein, Born was targeted by the Nazi regime, which dismissed him from his post in 1933. Born and his

Max Born described the wave function of a particle in mathematical terms.

family fled to England, where Born eventually accepted a permanent position at the University of Edinburgh. He remained there until his retirement in 1953. Afterward he and his wife resettled in West Germany.

In 1954, Born won the Nobel Prize in Physics for his research in quantum mechanics and his development of the wave function. During his acceptance speech, Born—no doubt recalling the Nazi scourge—remarked, "It is my greatest hope that the modern trend to subjugate science to politics and to inhuman ends and to erect barriers of fear and suspicion around national groups of scientists will not continue. For it is against the spirit of scientific research, as the mind can grow and bear fruit only in freedom."

Born died on January 5, 1970. He was eighty-seven years old. His final resting place is in the same cemetery as Max Planck.

ERWIN SCHRÖDINGER (1887–1961)

Erwin Schrödinger used de Broglie's theories on wave-particle duality to formulate a wave equation that correctly calculated the energy level of an electron in an atom. Schrödinger also developed a famous thought experiment called Schrödinger's Cat. This thought experiment presents a sort of paradoxical situation: If a cat is placed in a box with something that could kill the cat, no one would know if the cat was dead or alive until the box was open. Thus, until the box was open, the cat was in some sense both dead and alive. However, opening the door disrupts the nature of the experiment. Schrödinger likened this scenario to the problems inherent in presenting a theoretical reason for

Erwin Schrödinger formulated a wave equation that correctly calculated the energy level of an electron in an atom.

explaining why things happens. These problems are often found in quantum physics, which often relies on abstract theories rather than physical observations.

Schrödinger was born in Vienna, Austria, on August 12, 1887. His parents—Rudolf, who was a factory owner and a botanist, and Emily—had no other children. Schrödinger enjoyed skiing, skating, swimming, and mountain climbing.

In 1906, Schrödinger enrolled at the University of Vienna, where he studied physics. In 1910, he earned his doctorate degree. Schrödinger then worked as an assistant at the university until 1914, when he was drafted by the Austro-Hungarian military to serve as an artillery officer during the Great War. His tour of duty concluded with the defeat of the Central Powers (of which Austria-Hungary was one) in 1918.

Schrödinger married Annemarie (Anny) Bertel, the daughter of a respected chemist, in 1920. The couple enjoyed a long marriage—albeit an open one. Both Schrodinger and his wife blatantly engaged in multiple extramarital affairs. Schrödinger's wife bore him no children, but one of his mistresses did—a daughter named Ruth.

Schrödinger joined the faculty at the University of Zürich in 1921 and at the University of Berlin in 1927. In 1933, he received, along with Paul Dirac, the Nobel Prize in Physics for the discovery of new forms of atomic energy.

In 1933, Schrödinger, who had been raised Catholic but was by then an avowed atheist, resigned from his post at the University of Berlin to protest the Nazi regime. He then accepted a professorship at the University of Graz in Austria. After the 1938 Anschluss, in which Germany annexed Austria, Schrödinger found himself once again under German rule. This time he (along with his wife and mistress) fled to Ireland, where Schrödinger took a position at the Dublin Institute for Advanced Studies. He remained there for seventeen years.

Despite his contributions to the field, Schrödinger remained wary of the implications of quantum physics. "I don't like it," he once said, "and I'm sorry I ever had anything to do with it."

Schrödinger retired in 1956, and he returned to Vienna. He died of tuberculosis on January 4, 1961. He was seventy-three years old.

WOLFGANG PAULI (1900–1958)

Wolfgang Pauli developed the exclusion principle, or Pauli principle, which stated that no two electrons in an atom can occupy the same quantum state at the same time. Pauli also successfully predicted the existence of a subatomic particle called the neutrino.

Pauli was born on April 25, 1900, in Vienna, Austria. His parents were Wolfgang and Bertha. He had one sister. Pauli grew up among the intellectual elite of Vienna. Pauli's father came from a prominent Jewish family, but he became Roman Catholic shortly before his marriage.

In July 1921, Pauli earned a doctorate degree from the University of Munich. Two months later, he published his first paper, which pertained to Einstein's theory of general relativity. Einstein praised the paper. Between 1923 and 1930, Pauli held various positions at universities in Europe and the United States. Pauli won the Nobel Prize for Physics in 1925, for the discovery of the exclusion principle.

Pauli married a Berlin dancer named Käthe Deppner in 1929. They split just one year later. This event—coupled with the death of his mother by suicide three years earlier—persuaded Pauli to seek treatment from a famous psychologist named Carl Gustav Jung. Pauli remained close with Jung even after his treatment ended in 1934. That same year Pauli married Franziska Bertram, who worked for a Russian orchestra. The couple had no children.

The growing Nazi threat drove Pauli to emigrate to the United States, where he accepted a position at Princeton University working alongside Albert Einstein. He remained at Princeton until the end of the war, returning to Europe in 1946. He settled in Switzerland, where he remained until his death.

Throughout his career, Pauli enjoyed lively dialogues with his fellow scientists, including Einstein, Bohr, and others. He was also known for assisting other scientists with their work. Thanks to his critical judgments, which were generally sharp and to the point, he became known as "the conscience of physics."

In 1958, Pauli fell ill with pancreatic cancer. He died in Zürich, Switzerland, on December 15, 1958.

WERNER HEISENBERG (1901–1976)

Werner Heisenberg applied matrices to quantum physics. He also developed the Heisenberg uncertainty principle, which states that it is impossible to measure both the position and the momentum of a quantum at the same time.

Heisenberg was born on December 5, 1901, in Würzburg, Germany. His parents were Kaspar, who was a teacher, and Annie. As a boy Heisenberg enjoyed participating in the Neupfadfinder, which was similar to the Boy Scouts. He also played piano.

Heisenberg displayed a talent for mathematics early on. In 1920, he enrolled at the University of Munich, earning his doctorate degree three years later. For a time, Heisenberg worked at the University of Göttingen as an assistant to Max Born. He also completed a fellowship under the tutelage of Niels Bohr in Copenhagen. In 1928, Heisenberg accepted a professorship at the University of Leipzig.

Heisenberg—who, along with Max Born and Wolfgang Pauli, coined the term *quantenmechanik*, German for "quantum mechanics," which is another term for "quantum physics"—won the Nobel Prize in Physics in 1932 for the creation of quantum mechanics and the discovery of various hydrogen allotropes. (An allotrope is a variant form of an element. For example, a diamond is an allotrope of carbon.)

In 1937, Heisenberg married Elisabeth Schumacher, whom he met at a music recital. The couple raised seven children.

The rise of the Nazi Party placed Heisenberg in a difficult position. He was not a Nazi, but he loved his country. He felt obligated to remain there, even when the Nazis banned his Jewish colleagues from working in Germany and attacked Heisenberg himself for teaching theories developed by Jewish scientists. Eventually the Nazis reversed their opinion of Heisenberg and appointed him as leader of Germany's nuclear weapons project. (The Nazis failed to develop an atomic bomb.)

Paul Dirac (*left*) built on Werner Heisenberg's (*right*) matrix formulation of quantum mechanics.

In May 1945, Allied forces captured Heisenberg and detained him in England. After his release in January 1946, Heisenberg returned to Germany. He served as director for the Kaiser Wilhelm Institute for Physics until 1970. Heisenberg also served as the chairman of the Commission for Atomic Physics for the German Research Council and of the Nuclear Physics Working Group of the German Atomic Energy Commission.

Heisenberg died of cancer on February 1, 1976. He was seventy-four years old.

PAUL DIRAC (1902–1984)

Paul Dirac is best known for formulating a wave equation that unified quantum physics and special relativity to describe the behavior of certain subatomic particles. Dirac also correctly predicted the existence of new particles called antimatter.

Dirac was born the second of three children in Bristol, England, on August 8, 1902. Dirac's father, a Swiss immigrant named Charles, taught French. His mother, Florence, worked as a librarian. Paul had one sister and one brother.

Dirac earned degrees in electrical engineering (1921) and mathematics (1923) at the University of Bristol. After that he studied general relativity and quantum physics at St. Johns College at Cambridge, completing his doctorate degree in 1926. Dirac remained at Cambridge as a member of the faculty until 1969.

In 1933, Dirac shared the Nobel Prize for Physics with Erwin Schrödinger for the discovery of new forms of atomic energy. Physicists universally believe Dirac's achievements put him on par with the greats—scientists like Newton, Maxwell, and Einstein.

Dirac was famously withdrawn. Biographer Graham Farmelo described him using terms like "aloof," "determined," "literal-minded," "passive," "reticent," "shy," and "taciturn," noting that he lacked "social sensitivity." Nevertheless, in 1937, Dirac married Margit Wigner, whose brother Eugene was a gifted physicist. Dirac adopted Margit's son and daughter, and the couple had two daughters of their own.

A year into their marriage, Dirac uncharacteristically wrote to Margit, "You have made me human. I shall be able to live happily with you even if I have no more success in my work."

During World War II, Dirac remained at Cambridge, but a call from his government forced a change in his studies. Dirac quickly switched from investigating subatomic particles to satisfy his own curiosity to considering how to design and build a nuclear bomb.

In 1969, the Cambridge physics department revoked Dirac's parking space. This outraged Margit. At her insistence, Dirac accepted a fellowship at Florida State University (FSU) in 1970. Dirac remained at Florida State University until his death on October 20, 1984. He was eighty-two years old.

$b_x / x\rangle$

$+b_{/2}$

$\int_{b}^{b} dx \frac{1}{2} = L \cdot \frac{1}{2} = 1$

$x | \phi_{x'} \rangle$

$x) \Big|$

$x !$

$\doteq 0; h \neq h'$

$a \gtrsim 10^{-18} m$

$\longrightarrow x$

$\Psi_u(x) = \frac{1}{\sqrt{2L}} e^{i\gamma_0}\left(e^{i\left(\frac{2\pi}{L}u + h_0\right.}\right.$

$= \frac{2}{\sqrt{2L}} e^{i\gamma_u} \cos\left[\left(\frac{2\pi}{L}u + h\right.\right.$

$\Rightarrow \left(\frac{2\pi}{L}u + h_0\right)\frac{L}{2} = \frac{\pi}{2}(2\ell - 1)$

$\Psi_u(x) = \sqrt{\frac{2}{L}} \cos\left[\frac{\pi}{L}(2u - 1)x\right] \; ; \; \Psi_a-$

$\hat{H}\Psi_{us}(x) = -\frac{\hbar^2}{2m}\partial x^2 \Psi_{us}(x) =$

$E_{us} = \frac{\hbar^2}{2m}\frac{\pi^2}{L^2}(2u - 1)^2 \; ,$

$\hat{H}\Psi_a = -\frac{\hbar^2}{2m}\partial x^2 \Psi_G(x) = \frac{\hbar^2}{2m}$

$= -\frac{\hbar^2}{2m}\left(-\frac{1}{2a^2} + \left(\frac{1}{2a^2}(x-x_0)\right.\right.$

$\hat{H} \to \hat{H} = -\frac{\hbar^2}{2m}\partial \hat{x}^2 + V(\hat{x}) \; ;$

$V(x) = \frac{1}{2}m\omega^2(x - x_0)^2 \to m\omega^2 = \frac{}{}$

$\frac{1}{2}m\omega^2\hat{x}^2$

$R \; ; \; 2 (a\hat{p} + ib\hat{x})(a\hat{p} - ib\hat{x}), \; a, b \in R \longrightarrow$

$\ldots a^2\hat{p}^2 + b^2$

$a^2\hat{p}^2 + b$

$a^2 = \langle x -$

$; \; a^2 = \frac{}{2m} \; ; \; b^2 = \frac{}{2}m\omega$

$\frac{1}{\hbar\omega}(a\hat{p} - ib\hat{x}) \Rightarrow \hat{H} = \hbar\omega c^+ c$

$+ \frac{1}{2}\hbar\omega$

$\gtrsim \langle 3 \quad A \longrightarrow \omega \bar{A}\omega^{-1}$

Many concepts in quantum physics are quite complicated — as evidenced by this equation!

CHAPTER 4

Key Concepts in Quantum Mechanics

Quantum physics is an extremely complex field. To fully understand it requires years of study, and even then, comprehension remains elusive. Indeed, a Nobel laureate named Richard Feynman (1918–1988) once observed, "I think I can safely say that no one understands quantum mechanics." Another, Niels Bohr, remarked, "if you aren't confused by quantum mechanics, you haven't really understood it." Nevertheless, it is possible to grasp the key concepts of quantum physics, which are discussed in this chapter.

ATOMIC BEHAVIOR

Scientists believe everything in the universe—including macroscopic objects of all sizes—obeys the laws of quantum physics. But the study of quantum physics focuses primarily on matter at the atomic and subatomic level. This focus on the microscopic world has resulted in a complete overhaul of the atomic model.

Prior to quantum mechanics, physicist J. J. Thomson, who discovered the electron, posited that atoms were made of a positively charged substance containing negatively charged electrons. Thomson likened it to plum pudding—hence this model's name: the plum pudding model.

In 1911, physicist Ernest Rutherford concluded that atoms in fact consisted of a positively charged core, called a nucleus, surrounded by negatively charged electrons that orbited the nucleus in a circular manner, much the way planets orbit the sun. As far as Rutherford could tell, the distance of each orbital path from the nucleus was arbitrary. There was one problem with the Rutherford model: classical physics dictated that the electron would release energy by orbiting. This loss of energy would cause the electron to spiral ever inward and eventually collapse into the nucleus. Atoms in this model would therefore be extremely unstable.

In 1913, Danish physicist Niels Bohr applied quantum physics to the Rutherford model. Bohr theorized that the orbital path of an electron wasn't an arbitrary distance from the nucleus; rather, each electron orbited the nucleus at a specific radius. Bohr also posited that electrons could instantaneously jump from one distinct orbit to another, which is called a quantum jump. When a quantum jump occurred, Bohr surmised, the atom would either absorb energy or emit energy (depending on whether the electron jumped outward or inward, respectively).

Not to be outdone, Ernest Rutherford updated Bohr's model of the atom in 1920 to include an additional subatomic particle. This particle, which Rutherford called a proton, existed inside the nucleus of the atom, and it carried a positive charge. Physicist James Chadwick (1891–1974) discovered a second particle inside the nucleus in 1932. This one, called a neutron, carried no charge. (The number of protons in the nucleus of an atom is equal to the atom's atomic number. This number is used to classify each type of atom in the periodic table, which lists and categorizes all known chemical elements.)

Since then, scientists have hypothesized or discovered even smaller particles, called elementary particles. Scientists have identified several types of elementary particles, each type with its own mass (which, in some cases, is zero), charge, and spin. (Spin is a type of angular, as opposed to linear, momentum.) These particles are categorized into two main groups: fermions and bosons.

Fermions, which are named after an Italian physicist named Enrico Fermi, are generally described as matter particles, meaning that they serve as the foundation of all matter. There are four main types of fermions: quarks and leptons, as well as antiquarks and antileptons. (Antiquarks and antileptons are examples of antiparticles. Every type of subatomic particle is associated with an antiparticle, which has the same mass and spin as its counterpart but with the opposite charge.)

There are two groups of quarks based on their spin. The first group consists of three types of up-type quarks (up quarks, charm quarks, and top quarks) while the second group contains three types of down-type quarks (down quarks, strange quarks, and bottom quarks). Leptons, too, are categorized into two groups: charged (electron, muon, and tau) and neutral (electron neutrino, muon neutrino, and tau neutrino). As mentioned, each of these particles has its own antiparticle.

Unlike fermions, which are matter particles, bosons—named for Indian physicist Satyendra Nath Bose—are force particles. As such, they mediate interactions among fermions. Examples of bosons include gluons (associated with the strong force), photons (associated with the electromagnetic force), and Z bosons and W bosons (associated with the weak force). (You'll learn more about these forces later in this chapter.) All these bosons are categorized into a single group, called gauge bosons. In addition to these is one more type of boson: the Higgs boson. (Again, each of these particles has its own antiparticle.) In addition to gauge bosons and the Higgs boson, scientists postulate the existence of one more type of boson: the graviton, which would be associated with the gravitational force. So far, however, scientists have been unable to prove such a particle exists.

Both fermions and bosons can combine to form compound particles. Examples of compound particles include baryons (made of three quarks) and mesons (composed of one quark and one antiquark), both of which are also called hadrons. Other examples include positroniums (made of an electron and its antiparticle, called a positron), nucleons (also made of three quarks; protons and neutrons, which comprise the nucleus of an atom, are types of nucleons), and even whole atoms. Compound particles can behave like fermions or bosons, depending on their composition.

Scientists have developed a framework called the Standard Model to classify the various elementary particles. This framework also predicts how these particles interact and describes three of the four fundamental types of force

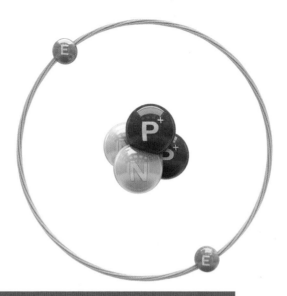

Early quantum physicists devised a new atomic model, which included a nucleus composed of protons and neutrons, circled by electrons.

fields (electromagnetic, weak, and strong). The Standard Model has helped scientists predict (and later confirm) the existence of several new particles.

QUANTA and FIELDS

Quantum physics describes the universe as consisting of quanta and fields. A quantum describes a specific amount of field energy that is highly unified and extended through space. Physicists believe that quanta make up everything in the universe—from fermions, protons, neutrons, electrons, atoms, molecules, and photons to planets, stars, and galaxies, and everything in between. Quantum physics, then, is about the nature and behavior of these quanta.

The CERN Large Hadron Collider

In 2008, the European Organization for Nuclear Research (CERN) completed construction of the Large Hadron Collider (LHC), the largest and most powerful particle collider in the world.

The LHC, located near Geneva, Switzerland, consists of a circular underground tunnel that is seventeen miles (twenty-seven kilometers) around. The tunnel contains particle accelerators, which fling subatomic particles through the tunnel at very high speeds. When these particles collide with other particles, the resulting collisions enable scientists to confirm (or not) the existence of theoretical subatomic particles and perhaps even predict the existence of completely new ones.

Experts describe the LHC, which employs thousands of physicists from all over the world, as the most complex contraption ever constructed. Indeed, the LHC generates enough data per second to fill more than one thousand one-terabyte hard drives.

In 2012, scientists at the LHC announced they had observed a particle whose existence had been predicted in 1960. This particle, called a Higgs boson, is described as a fundamental building block

The CERN LHC has been described as one of the most complex contraptions ever constructed.

of the universe. A Higgs boson, known as a force carrier, mediates the interactions of other types of fundamental particles called fermions. In doing so, the Higgs boson gives all matter its mass. It's impossible to overstate the significance of this discovery. Indeed, for many physicists, it's the final piece of the puzzle that represents our current grasp of the nature of our universe.

Quanta have some striking characteristics. One characteristic is that they either exist in their entirety or they don't exist at all. They're all or nothing. There is no in between. This has two important ramifications. First, quanta are unified. They cannot under any circumstance be divided. Second, they cannot be gradually created or destroyed. The creation or destruction of a quantum happens instantaneously. (In addition to being created or destroyed instantaneously, quanta also instantaneously change quantum states.)

Another characteristic is that quanta are *not* particles—although they sometimes act like them. (This characteristic is called wave-particle duality and is discussed in the next section.) That is, they do not exist at any single point. Rather, they extend through space.

A third characteristic is that quanta are changeable and unpredictable. They can exist in several quantum states. For example, they can be infinitesimal or enormous. They can shrink or expand. They contain lots of energy or not so much. They can exist at any location and move in any direction. They can also—and this is weird—exist in two or more of these different states *at the same time*. This phenomenon is called superposition. (Superposition is discussed later in this chapter.)

Quanta aren't things, exactly. Rather, a quantum is a wave in a field. Just as a wave of water is not a separate thing from the water in which it moves, a quantum is part of the field in which it exists. So, when we say everything in the universe is made entirely of quanta, what we really mean is that the universe is made entirely of fields.

Fields exist at every point in a specific region of space.

Unlike a quantum, a field is a thing—one that exists at every point in a specific region of space. There are different types of fields, including force fields and matter fields. Force fields come in four varieties (although scientists believe these may in fact be components of a single unified force). One type of force field is the gravitational field. This field is what keeps planets like Earth in orbit around their sun. The gravitational field also gets credit for the formation of stars and galaxies. Another type of field is the electromagnetic field. This field is behind phenomena like light, heat, electricity, and magnetism. It's also what holds atoms together. Then, there are the strong field and the weak field. The strong field is responsible for holding the innards of the nucleus in an atom—its protons and neutrons—together and, by extension, for the stability of matter. Finally, the weak field, which also acts inside the nucleus of an atom, is the force behind certain types of radioactive decay. For their part, matter fields consist of six lepton fields, six quark fields, and the electron field. There is also a Higgs field. Together all these fields consume all of space.

WAVE-PARTICLE DUALITY

Chapter 2 discussed the double-slit experiment conducted in 1801 by British scientist Thomas Young. To review, Young projected light rays from a single concentrated source through two thin slits onto a screen. As the light passed through the slits, it created an interference pattern on the screen, indicating that the light traveled in waves rather

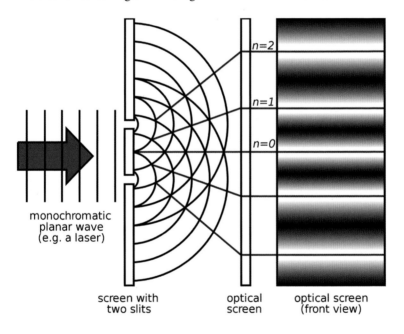

monochromatic
planar wave
(e.g. a laser)

$n=2$

$n=1$

$n=0$

screen with
two slits

optical
screen

optical screen
(front view)

The two-slit experiment revealed the wave-particle duality of light.

than particles. However, the interference pattern itself was composed of tiny points on the screen, suggesting that sometimes light acted like particles—a behavior that came to be known as Compton scattering. This phenomenon is called wave-particle duality.

In 1923, physicist Louis de Broglie posited that if light (or more generally radiation) exhibited wave-particle duality, then matter should too. To prove this hypothesis, scientists conducted double-slit experiments on matter such as molecules, protons, neutrons, and electrons. The results of these experiments led them to conclude that de Broglie was correct. Wave-particle duality has many interesting implications, including fundamental randomness, superposition, quantum entanglement, and quantum tunneling. These are discussed next.

FUNDAMENTAL RANDOMNESS

Suppose you conduct a double-slit experiment with an electron. Because the electron acts like a wave, there's no way to predict where on the screen the electron will strike. You can only say where it might strike. Therefore, electron waves—indeed all waves of matter and light—are in fact probability waves. This means that, unlike classical physics, which is deterministic and predictable in nature (like a mechanical clock), quantum physics is probabilistic.

One can precisely measure the exact position and momentum (velocity) of a particle. But quanta exist in wave form, and the very nature of a wave makes it impossible to pin down these values for a quantum—at least, not both at the same time. This is called the Heisenberg uncertainty principle. This principle, articulated by Werner Heisenberg, states that although it is possible to measure a wave's position or its momentum, it is impossible to measure both at once. Moreover, the more accurately you measure one of these values, the less accurately you can measure the other. To return to the double-slit experiment with the electron, this inability to obtain both these measurements at the same time explains why it's impossible to predict where on the screen the electron will strike.

The probabilistic nature of quantum physics has one important implication: Nature is fundamentally random. In other words, there is absolutely nothing in nature that dictates whether one quantum will interact with another. If two (or more) quanta do interact, there is absolutely nothing in nature that dictates what the outcome of that interaction will be. But because quantum physics is probabilistic, scientists can determine the probability that two (or more quanta) will interact and, if they do, the outcome of that interaction. These probabilities are expressed in something called a wave function. For example, in the case of the electron in the double-slit experiment, the wave function contains all possible points on the screen where the electron might strike it. When the electron actually strikes the screen, the wave function is said to collapse. (Note that although nature is random, this does not mean quantum physics is without rules. Indeed, physicists have established several precise, rational, and consistent rules that apply within the quantum framework, including Heisenberg's uncertainty principle.)

Interestingly, some physicists believe the universe is not random—rather, it merely seems so because scientists have failed to identify and measure all necessary variables. Einstein counted himself among these dissenters, famously arguing that "God does not play dice." The existence of these so-called hidden variables implies that quantum physics is incomplete. Most physicists have rejected this hypothesis, however.

SUPERPOSITION

In addition to fundamental randomness, wave-function duality and the probabilistic nature of quanta also result in a phenomenon called superposition. The superposition principle states that if a quantum can exist in any one of multiple different states, it can exist in all of those states simultaneously. This suggests that lacking information about what state a quantum is in, one can assume it is in all possible states—take all possible paths—at once and will remain so until the wave function of the quantum collapses.

If you think this sounds crazy, you're in good company. Einstein agreed with you, and so did Erwin Schrödinger. Schrödinger's thought experiment called Schrödinger's Cat highlighted the absurdity of superposition. In this experiment, Schrödinger imagined sealing a living cat inside a box. Schrödinger then imagined that the box also contained one atom of a radioactive material that was as likely to decay as not, a Geiger counter (for measuring radioactive radiation) rigged to a hammer, and a glass flask of poison gas. If the atom of radioactive material did in fact decay, it would trigger a chain reaction: the atom would emit radioactive radiation; the Geiger counter would detect the radiation; the rigging mechanism would release the hammer;

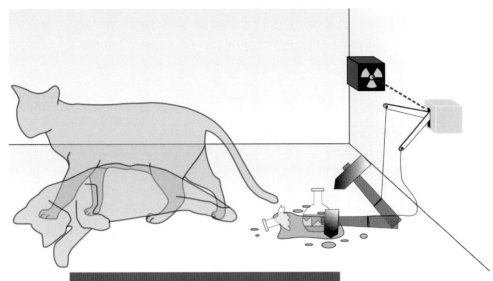

This diagram explains the Schrödinger's Cat thought experiment.

and the hammer would break the glass flask. This would release the poison gas and kill the (imaginary) cat. If the atom did not decay, then the chain of events that resulted in the release of the poison gas would not occur, and the (imaginary) cat would remain alive. Here's where the thought experiment got interesting: Schrödinger asserted that the principle of superposition indicated that until someone opened the box to observe the cat and measure the atom's radioactivity (akin to a wave function collapsing), the cat would be both dead and alive at the same time. This, Schrödinger believed, was absurd.

Yet, scientist have observed superposition—at least at the quantum level. Indeed, it happens all the time at the microscopic level. Moreover, the rules of quantum physics indicate that superposition can happen—albeit not without difficulty—at the macroscopic level too.

Accepting Quantum Oddities

Clearly quantum physics describes behavior that seems contrary to that observed in the macroscopic world. For example, consider superposition. No single object in the macroscopic world appears to assume multiple states or move along multiple paths simultaneously. Surely that means it's impossible for a single quantum to do it. Yet, a quantum can assume multiple states or move along multiple paths simultaneously, and scientists have shown that it does.

Scientists dream up some strange ideas. However, the scientific method prevents them from putting those ideas forward as "fact" (or at least as close to a "fact" as a thing can be) without rigorous experimentation and testing. Scientists also ascribe to a principle called Occam's razor. This principle states that when faced with a scientific conundrum, such as the behavior of a quantum, one should assume the simplest answer is correct. If, through observation and experimentation, one concludes that the simplest answer is not correct, one should pursue the next simplest answer, and so on. All this is to say that scientists maintain that a quantum can assume multiple states or move along multiple paths simultaneously because all the simpler answers didn't check out.

Still, readers can take comfort in knowing that even physicists struggle with these oddities. Following a presentation by physicist Wolfgang Pauli on a new quantum theory of elementary particles, Niels Bohr told him, "We are all agreed that your theory is crazy. The question that divides us is whether it is crazy enough to have a chance of being correct."

QUANTUM ENTANGLEMENT

Superposition occurs when one quantum exhibits multiple states at the same time. Quantum entanglement describes when two (or more) quanta become joined together and behave in a highly correlated manner. When this happens the two (or more) quanta behave much like a single unified quantum—that is, when two (or more) quanta are entangled, the state of one quantum will match exactly the state of the other quantum at all times. Moreover, if the state of one of these quanta changes, the state of the other will also—instantaneously. This is true even if the quanta exist light-years apart from each other, indicating that these simultaneous changes aren't the result of some type of faster-than-light-speed signaling between the two quanta. This phenomenon is often called non-locality.

Einstein (among others) was skeptical of quantum entanglement. Indeed, he described it as "spooky action at a distance." It's true that quantum entanglement does seem to fly in the face of several key principles of classical physics—rules like Einstein's theory of special relativity, which asserts that nothing can travel faster than the speed of light, and the notion that objects can be influenced only by their immediate surroundings. Even those scientists who do not dismiss quantum entanglement out of hand are at a loss to understand how entangled quanta know what their "twin" is doing. Nevertheless, physicists have proved the existence of quantum entanglement mathematically.

QUANTUM TUNNELING

In Schrödinger's thought experiment, he imagined a cat inside a box containing an atom of radioactive material. Whether the cat ultimately lived or died depended on whether the radioactive atom decayed. Perhaps you're wondering what causes this decay.

Radioactive decay occurs when the nucleus in an unstable, or radioactive, atom loses energy by ejecting a certain type of subatomic particle. There are a few types of radioactive decay, but the one that is significant here is alpha decay. With alpha decay, a subatomic particle called an alpha particle, which resides inside the nucleus of an atom, tunnels through the membrane of the nucleus to break through to the other side. (An alpha particle consists of two protons and two neutrons bound together.)

At first scientists found alpha decay puzzling for one simple reason: alpha particles lacked sufficient energy to break through the nucleic membrane. In 1928, a scientist named George Gamow (1904–1968) concluded that this behavior, which he called quantum tunneling, was a natural by-product of the alpha particle's wave properties.

To understand this, imagine an alpha particle is a ball at the bottom of a mound, and you want to roll it up and over the mound to the other side. According to classical physics, if you lack the strength to roll the ball up and over, it will simply roll back down to you. But in quantum physics, a ball, which generally behaves like a particle, has wave properties.

So, rather than imagining the ball rolling over the mound (the way a particle might), imagine it clearing the mound the way a high jumper clears the bar. The high jumper's head (one part of the wave) clears the bar first, followed by her back (another part of the wave), and eventually her feet (yet another part of the wave). In this way, the energy of the high jumper (or the ball or the alpha particle) can be lower than that needed to push through a barrier and yet gradually transfer itself past it.

Radioactive decay is just one example of quantum tunneling in action. Quantum tunneling is also the driving behavior behind such natural phenomena as photosynthesis (the process by which plants convert light energy to chemical energy) and the spontaneous mutation of DNA. Perhaps most notably, quantum tunneling plays a key role in nuclear fusion—a nuclear reaction that causes our sun (and most other stars) to shine.

The THEORY of EVERYTHING

As promising as quantum physics is, it is not without problems. Indeed, more than a century after Max Planck identified the quantized nature of energy as the cause of blackbody radiation, scientists hotly contest certain fundamental areas in quantum physics.

One of these disputes pertains to measurement, which is discussed in chapter 5. Another dispute centers around Einstein's theory of general relativity. Not only does this theory fail to take quantum physics into account, but it is wholly incompatible with it. Further, although scientists have confirmed through rigorous experimentation virtually every prediction made by both fields of study—general relativity and quantum physics—to a high degree of accuracy, they have yet to reconcile this incompatibility (pertaining primarily to the issue of gravity) between them. Perhaps this is in part because quantum physics applies to the very small (subatomic particles, atoms, and so forth), while the theory of general relativity is all about the very big (stars and galaxies).

One disconnect between the two disciplines pertains to the four fundamental forces: gravitational, electromagnetic, strong, and weak. The principles laid forth by Einstein's theory of general relativity govern the gravitational force. The other three forces—electromagnetic, strong, and weak—are dictated by quantum physics. Another issue is that general relativity (and, more broadly, classical physics) asserts that one can precisely predict the behavior of an object, while in quantum physics, one is limited to calculating the probability that an object will behave a certain way.

For decades, scientists have sought one single theory to unify quantum physics and general relativity (and maybe classical physics too). This theory, which scientists cheekily dubbed the theory of everything (perhaps not expecting the name to stick), would describe everything. It would describe stars and planets and galaxies, and quarks and electrons and atoms, and everything in between. This theory (assuming scientists ever piece it together) will be a "final" theory, meaning there will be nothing left in physics to discover.

For a time, it seemed the articulation of such a theory was imminent. Indeed, in 1980, physicist Stephen Hawking predicted the theory could be complete by the year 2000.

But as of this writing, no such theory is forthcoming. Still, scientists have a few different ideas on what might constitute a theory of everything.

One such idea is called string theory. This theory assumes all quanta are in fact identical strings. These strings are under tension, like strings on a guitar, and vibrate at different frequencies depending on their size. The frequency at which a string vibrates dictates what kind of particle the string is. For example, a string vibrating at one frequency might be an electron; a string vibrating at a different frequency might be a proton; and so on. String theory also proposes the existence of additional dimensions beyond the three dimensions of space and the one dimension of time.

This theory appears to make sense of all forces in nature—electromagnetic, gravitational, strong, and weak. But scientists don't yet understand every aspect of string theory, nor do they have a clear way to articulate it—verbally or mathematically. (Scientists say the math involved in string theory is so mind-boggling that the field of mathematics in its current state is barely capable of describing it.) As a result, scientists have in fact developed not one version of string theory but several—each one quite different from the others.

A different theory, called M-theory, unifies the various versions of string theory into a single model. M-theory predicts the existence of eleven total dimensions. Scientists envision these dimensions as existing as extended regions called membranes, or branes for short, with each brane being sufficiently large to contain an entire universe. M-theory suggests that these branes are arranged together much like papers in a sheaf, comprising a multiverse.

M-theory neatly unites quantum physics and relativity. It even explains the Big Bang by asserting that the massive explosion that scientists believe resulted in the formation of our universe was caused by a collision between one or more branes. At present M-theory is incomplete, and no experimental support for the theory exists. However, the underlying mathematics check out—making it, said Stephen Hawking, "the only candidate for a complete theory of the universe."

That's not to say that Hawking believed M-theory is in fact the theory of everything. Quite the contrary. He simply meant that if it turns out there is such a theory, then it's likely M-theory will be it. But over the years, Hawking, like many other physicists, grew increasingly skeptical that such a theory is in fact possible. In other words, maybe nature just doesn't unify. Hawking explained: "This radical theory holds that there doesn't exist, even in principle, a single comprehensive theory of the universe. Instead, science offers many incomplete windows onto a common reality, one no more 'true' than another."

Lasers are just one technology made possible by developments in our understanding of quantum mechanics.

CHAPTER 5

Quantum Mechanics Today

Quantum physics has revolutionized our understanding of the world and brought innovative technologies that touch every aspect of our lives. One such technology is the laser. Surveyors and construction workers use lasers for measurement and alignment purposes. Doctors employ lasers to burn away tissue, cauterize cuts, stop bleeding, correct vision, break up kidney stones, aid in delicate surgeries, treat skin conditions, and remove wrinkles. Machinists use lasers to cut, drill, or weld hard materials. (Lasers are also great for entertaining cats.)

Other examples of technology made possible by the study of quantum physics include magnetic resonance imaging (MRI), which uses radio waves and magnetic fields to generate images of organs inside a body, and the Global Positioning System (GPS), which employs a network of satellites to provide users with information as to their geographic position.

The Measurement Problem

Not every aspect of quantum physics is settled. For example, one problem, called the measurement problem, has followed physicists for nearly a century. This problem stems from the fact that measurements in quantum physics do not yield definite outcomes but instead result in a series of probabilities.

It also pertains to the fact that measuring a quantum system often disturbs that system, which affects the resulting measurement. Both phenomena make it difficult to glean the true state and nature of a quantum.

Some scientists believe the measurement problem cannot be solved by quantum physics, meaning our understanding of quantum physics is wrong. Others say the measurement problem can be solved by quantum physics, meaning our understanding of quantum physics is correct but incomplete. Still others claim the measurement problem isn't really a problem at all because the field of quantum physics is merely an abstract concept.

A few scientists offer a more fanciful explanation: the many-worlds interpretation. This interpretation, proposed by physicist Hugh Everett III (1930–1982) in 1957, suggests that measurements in quantum physics are neither probabilistic nor random. Instead, each possible value for a measurement exists in its own separate branch of reality.

For example, imagine measuring an electron in a superposition of two states—position A and position B. In one branch of reality you perceive the electron to be at position A, but in another, at position B. Each "version" of you perceives itself to be unique and assumes the position of the electron is random. But in fact, there are versions of you for every possible position—none, says Everett, "any more 'real' than the rest." So, while we often characterize mathematics as objective and certain, we find that it can often lead to some challenges and uncertainties, at least when it comes to quantum mechanics.

This chapter focuses on two other revolutionary technologies brought about by the study of quantum physics: nuclear fission and the transistor. This chapter also introduces readers to two other technologies still under development: quantum computing and quantum cryptography. Finally, it notes numerous new disciplines that have emerged since the discovery of quantum physics.

NUCLEAR FISSION and the ADVENT of the ATOMIC AGE

By the 1930s, physicists had learned a great deal about the structure of atoms. Armed with this knowledge, several scientists, including a female physicist named Lise Meitner (1878–1968), conducted experiments that involved bombarding uranium atoms with neutrons. They discovered that this bombardment of neutrons split the nucleus inside the uranium atom in half. This in turn resulted in an emission of particles from inside the nucleus of the uranium atom (including neutrons), the formation of a barium atom, and the release of a significant amount of energy—a process that became known as nuclear fission.

In 1939, Hungarian physicist Leó Szilárd (1898–1964) recognized that nuclear fission could unleash a self-sustaining chain reaction. In other words, a fission reaction could emit neutrons, and those neutrons could in turn trigger a new fission reaction. But that wasn't all. Szilárd also concluded that if the fission of one nucleus released more than one neutron, the number of ensuing fission reactions could grow exponentially. The end result of this exponential

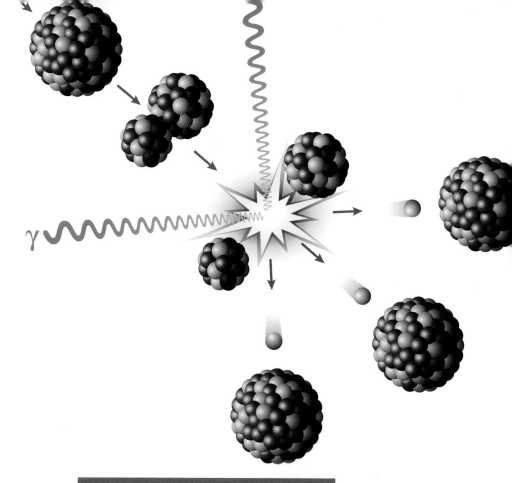

γ

Nuclear chain reactions are series of nuclear fissions, each started by a neutron produced in a prior fission.

chain reaction would be the release of massive amounts of energy. In December 1942, a scientist named Enrico Fermi (1901–1954) confirmed Szilárd's hypothesis by constructing the first operational nuclear reactor, which he called an atomic pile, under the football field at the University of Chicago, in Chicago, Illinois.

One obvious use for this nuclear chain reaction was to generate clean and sustainable electric power. This power could illuminate entire cities, fuel vehicles ranging from cars to submarines to space shuttles, drive production in factories, and more—without casting a single iota of carbon based airborne pollution into the atmosphere. The next several decades heralded the construction of nuclear power plants all over the world. Today, these plants—some 448 in all—generate about 11 percent of the world's electricity.

Most scientists contend that nuclear power is a safe and sustainable energy source that produces virtually no air pollution. However, many people oppose its use, claiming it poses a serious threat to the health of humans and the environment. Antinuclear activists cite nuclear accidents such as those at Three Mile Island in 1979, Chernobyl in 1986, and Fukushima in 2011, as well as the radioactive nuclear waste produced by the fission process.

Another obvious use of the chain reaction was to produce bombs of unparalleled destructive force. Given that Szilárd's discovery of nuclear fission coincided with the advent of World War II, this was particularly alarming. In 1939, Szilárd persuaded his friend Albert Einstein to write a series of letters to United States president Franklin D. Roosevelt to warn him of the danger. "It may become possible to set up a nuclear chain reaction in a large mass of uranium," Einstein wrote in one letter, "by which vast amounts of power and large quantities of new radium-like elements would be generated. This new phenomenon would also lead to the construction of bombs." The letter continued: "A single bomb of this type, carried by boat and exploded in a port, might very well destroy the whole port together with some of the surrounding territory." The letter closed by

Smoke from the world's first atom bomb hovered over Hiroshima, Japan, on August 6, 1945.

warning Roosevelt that there was reason to believe German scientists were already working to build such a bomb.

In 1942, at Roosevelt's behest, the United States Army Corps of Engineers assembled a group of top scientists to build a fission, or atomic, bomb. This massive undertaking was dubbed the Manhattan Project. By the summer of 1945, these scientists had successfully designed and constructed three such bombs. On July 16, 1945, scientists detonated the first one, which they dubbed Trinity, in the New Mexico desert. Pilots in the United States Air Force dropped the other two—called Little Boy and Fat Man—on the Japanese cities of Hiroshima and Nagasaki.

The bombing of Hiroshima and Nagasaki did hasten the end of World War II, but at a cost of untold death and destruction. The blast in Hiroshima alone, which occurred on August 6, 1945, vaporized more than 6 square miles

(10 sq km) of the city. Thousands upon thousands of its inhabitants— most of them civilians—were killed instantly. Some simply vanished due to the intense heat from the explosion. Those who survived the bomb's immediate impact perished in the blazing hot fires that plagued the city over the next three days or from the long-term effects of radiation exposure. The bombing of Nagasaki, on August 9, 1945, produced comparable results (but on a smaller scale). Experts estimate that these bombings combined killed more than two hundred thousand people—more than a third of the total population of both cities.

Today, eight countries are known to possess fission bombs: United States of America, Russia, United Kingdom, France, China, India, Pakistan, and North Korea. (Israel may also possess such weapons.) Some of these bombs are as much as eighty times more powerful than Little Boy. Were such a bomb to detonate over a densely populated area, millions would perish in the explosion or ensuing fires or from radiation exposure. The inevitable nuclear winter that followed would kill millions more. (Nuclear winter occurs because of the layer of smoke and dust, produced by the bomb, that would hover in the atmosphere over an extended time. This layer would block the sun, thereby preventing human populations from growing food.)

The TRANSISTOR and the AGE of INFORMATION

Nuclear winter is an example of a negative outcome of quantum physics. A positive outcome is the invention of the transistor. Created in 1947 by scientists at Bell

Laboratories, a transistor (a portmanteau of the words "transfer" and "resistor") is a type of semiconductor device that generates, controls, and amplifies an electrical signal. (A semiconductor is a kind of material through which an electrical current is transmitted.)

Transistors were developed to replace an earlier technology called a vacuum tube or electron tube. These tubes encased a near-vacuum to allow for the free flow of electrical current. By the 1940s, vacuum tubes had paved the way for the development of radio, television, radar, sound-recording devices, large telephone networks, and analog and digital computers. However, these tubes were notoriously bulky, slow, power-hungry, and fragile.

The transistor had two key advantages: it was small, and it didn't generate a lot of heat. This meant that you could pack a lot of them into a very small space without the whole apparatus going up in smoke. They performed well too, which meant they could do more than just replace a vacuum tube; they could do things a vacuum tube couldn't.

At first transistors were made from a material called germanium. This resulted in significant leakage of electrical current. During the 1950s, scientists developed a transistor made of another material called silicon. Because of its higher melting temperature, silicon was more difficult to work with than germanium. But it also had greater reactivity, meaning it could yield significantly better performance. (The use of silicon in transistors is why the famous tech hub in the San Francisco Bay Area is called Silicon Valley.)

Early applications of the transistor included hearing aids and pocket radios—made possible by the transistor's small size. During the 1960s and 1970s, scientists incorporated

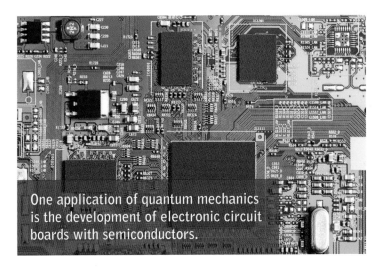

One application of quantum mechanics is the development of electronic circuit boards with semiconductors.

transistors into integrated circuits, or microchips, which are now used in electronics of all sorts. Since then scientists have developed increasingly smaller transistors to fit more of them onto a single chip. Today's chips—some roughly the size of a human fingernail—contain as many as several billion transistors, giving them millions of times the capacity and thousands of times the speed of their early predecessors.

Transistors permeate nearly every electronic device manufactured today. As such, they are the backbone of revolutionary new technologies, including personal computers, smartphones, and the World Wide Web. These technologies are in turn responsible for sweeping transformations in societies all over the world. Thanks to these technologies, people can disseminate information all over the world nearly instantaneously, and they can connect with friends, family, and customers everywhere on the earth. The result has been a seismic shift from localized economies to a global one—and, in the Western world, from an industrial-based economy to a knowledge-based one.

The PROMISE of QUANTUM COMPUTING

In traditional computing, data is encoded into binary digits called bits. Each bit can exist in just one of two possible states: as a one or a zero. Quantum computing—still in its infancy—is different. In quantum computing, data exists in quantum bits, or qubits. Each qubit can exist as a one, a zero, or both. In other words, a qubit could be in a superposition of both states. Encoding information into qubits enables quantum computers to process that information using quantum phenomena such as quantum tunneling and quantum entanglement. As a result, quantum computers could conceivably calculate certain problems in a matter of days rather than in a matter of years.

The quantum computer was conceived by Russian mathematician Yuri Manin (1937–) in 1980. Since then, several scientists and scientific organizations have worked tirelessly to build a fully functioning quantum computer. This has proven quite difficult for various reasons. One key design constraint is the need for qubits inside a quantum computer to maintain coherence for a sufficiently long time to actually perform a calculation. In the context of quantum physics, coherence pertains to the stability of an object's quantum state, which, as discussed, can change randomly.

Despite these and other constraints, the last few years have brought marked progress in the realization of the quantum computer. Indeed, in 2015, the National Aeronautics and Space Administration (NASA), in collaboration with Google and Universities Space Research Association (USRA), unveiled the world's first fully operational quantum computer, called the D-Wave 2X and boasting a whopping 1,097 qubits. In 2016, International

Business Machines Corporation (IBM) launched the
IBM Quantum Experience (QX), which makes quantum
computing available to anyone through the cloud. In 2017,
IBM announced an initiative to build a commercially
available quantum computer called the IBM Q, while
Microsoft developed a programming language called Q# to
enable developers to write programs for quantum computers.

The POWER of QUANTUM CRYPTOGRAPHY

Quantum computing has paved the way for another
important quantum application: the quantum cryptography
of digital information, including digital communications.

Classical cryptography uses a technology called RSA.
RSA works by making it as difficult as possible for an
unauthorized party to hack information or communications.
To achieve this, RSA relies on two keys, both of which
consist of very large number: a public key for encryption,
and a private, or secret, key for decryption. Anyone with
the public key can encrypt digital information. But only
someone with the private key can decrypt it.

While it's difficult to decrypt information without
the private key, it's not impossible—if you have enough
computing power at your disposal (for example, a
quantum computer). This explains why more and more
cryptographers have shifted their focus to using the laws of
quantum physics to ascertain new ways to send messages
that cannot be hacked. One result of this ongoing effort has

been the development of a new form of cryptography called quantum key distribution (QKD).

On the surface QKD works a lot like RSA. One key encodes a message, and another key decodes it. What is different is that QKD uses quantum states to transmit the message and the decoder key to the recipient. If a third party attempts to intercept the message and key, they will need to measure their quantum state in some way, which will inevitably disrupt it. In this way, the eavesdropper is detected, in which case the system either generates a new key and delivers the message or aborts the communication.

Quantum cryptologists have also explored the use of quantum entanglement to ensure secure communications. As discussed, quantum entanglement causes two (or more) separate quanta to behave like a single entity—even if they're quite far apart. This approach could enable users to securely send messages without the use of transmission media such as cables or wireless signals. This approach operates on the same principle as QKD: if someone attempts to intercept the message, they will inevitably disrupt its quantum state, thereby blowing their cover.

With respect to communications, quantum entanglement could also allow for the construction of a so-called quantum internet. This quantum internet would operate in the same distributed manner as the regular internet but would use entangled quanta rather than the aforementioned transmission to transmit data. The result would be super-secure, faster-than-light communications—a prospect that holds enormous appeal in an era in which cyberattacks continue to proliferate and lag time remains a frustration.

Quantum cryptography is still in its infancy. It may well be a while before it becomes commercially viable. But baby step by baby step, it's coming.

BRANCHING OUT

As scientists learn more and more about quantum physics, the field has branched into several distinct disciplines. One of these disciplines is quantum chemistry. Quantum chemistry is the application of the rules of quantum physics to the study of atoms and molecules. By using the rules of quantum physics, scientists can more accurately predict the structures of atoms and molecules as well as their behavior. They can also better explain the structure of the periodic table.

Another discipline is quantum electrodynamics (QED). QED describes the study of the behavior and interactions of photons and subatomic particles such as electrons and positrons. More precisely QED explores the electromagnetic processes behind the creation of these particles as well as the processes by which they are annihilated.

Related to both quantum chemistry and quantum electrodynamics is particle physics. Particle physics involves the study of the fundamental constituents of matter (particles like protons, neutrons, electrons, fermions, hadrons, and others) and how they are governed by the four fundamental forces (gravitational, electromagnetic, strong, and weak).

Quantum chemistry, quantum electrodynamics, and particle physics pertain to very small things. In contrast, cosmology—another discipline of quantum physics—is the study of the universe. It's true that much of cosmology centers around Einstein's theory of general relativity rather than quantum physics. But scientists do believe the origin of the universe—in other words, the Big Bang—involved quantum behavior.

CONCLUSION

While scientists originally believed that Newtonian physics correctly described our universe, today, scientists overwhelmingly believe that quantum physics achieves this. Still there remain those who aren't so sure. They cite myriad examples of "quantum weirdness" that seem to contradict common sense.

One such scientist is Nobel laureate Steven Weinberg. "Maybe it's just the way we express the theory is bad," Weinberg says, "and the theory itself is right." Or maybe, he says, "there's something else entirely." In other words, maybe "we're going to have a revolution in science which is as much of a break with the past as quantum mechanics is a break from classical physics."

Either way, it's an exciting time for science!

Chronology

1687   Sir Isaac Newton publishes the *Principia*, outlining three laws of motion and a law of gravity. These laws served as the foundation of physics for more than two hundred years.

1712   The steam engine is invented, revealing the relationship between heat and work.

1801   Thomas Young performs the double-slit experiment and proves that light exhibits wave-like behavior and particle-like behavior.

1803   John Dalton produces an atomic model that serves as the basis of our modern model.

1830s   Michael Faraday develops the concept of a field.

1847   Scientists state the first law of thermodynamics, which asserts that energy in a closed system can be neither created nor destroyed.

1865   James Clerk Maxwell summarizes the work of Faraday and others into a series of equations and publishes them in a treatise called *A Dynamical Theory of the Electromagnetic Field*.

1874   Scientists state the second law of thermodynamics, which asserts that entropy increases over time.

1887   Heinrich Hertz discovers the photoelectric effect.

1888   Hertz proves the existence of electromagnetic waves.

1897   J. J. Thomson discovers the electron.

1900   Max Planck solves the problem of blackbody radiation by hypothesizing that the energy inside atoms is quantized.

1905   Albert Einstein confirms Planck's hypothesis by solving the problem of the photoelectric effect and proposes the existence of the photon. Einstein presents his theory of special relativity.

1911   Ernest Rutherford discovers that all atoms contain a nucleus.

1913   Niels Bohr develops a new atomic model based on the laws of quantum physics.

1915   Albert Einstein presents his theory of general relativity.

1920   Rutherford discovers the proton.

1924   Louis de Broglie predicts the wave-like behavior of particles such as electrons and hypothesizes that all matter has wave properties. The first use of the term *quantenmechanik* (German for "quantum mechanics") appears in a publication by Max Born.

1925   Wolfgang Pauli determines that now two electrons
        in an atom can occupy the same quantum state at
        the same time (called the exclusion principle or the
        Pauli principle).

1926   Erwin Schrödinger formulates a wave equation that
        correctly calculates the energy level of an electron in
        an atom.

1927   Werner Heisenberg formulates his uncertainty
        principle, which states that it is impossible to
        measure both the position and the momentum of a
        quantum at the same time.

1928   Paul Dirac formulates a wave equation to describe
        the behavior of certain subatomic particles.

193   Dirac correctly predicts the existence of antimatter.

1932   James Chadwick discovers the neutron.

1933–1945
        The Nazis control Germany and conquer much of
        Europe. They force many quantum physicists from
        their homes.

1939   Leó Szilárd envisions the nuclear chain reaction
        called fission. United States president Franklin D.
        Roosevelt calls for the creation of the Manhattan
        Project, the name for the American effort to build a
        nuclear bomb.

1942   Enrico Fermi constructs the first nuclear reactor, which he calls an atomic pile.

1945   The United States completes the design and construction of three nuclear bombs. United States pilots drop two of these bombs on Japan to end World War II.

1947   Scientists at Bell Laboratories invent the transistor. This tiny invention transforms the world by ushering in the age of information.

1980   Russian mathematician Yuri Manin comes up with the idea of the quantum computer.

2002   Stephen Hawking publishes *The Theory of Everything: The Origin and Fate of the Universe*.

2015   The National Aeronautics and Space Administration (NASA), in collaboration with Google and Universities Space Research Association (USRA), reveals the world's first fully operational quantum computer.

Glossary

allotrope A variant form of an element.

autodidact A self-taught person.

blackbody A theoretical "perfect" surface that absorbs and emits all frequencies of thermal radiation.

boson A force particle.

cathode ray A beam of electrons emitted from the cathode of a high-vacuum tube.

classical physics Describes the discipline of physics before Max Planck's discovery of quantum physics. Also called Newtonian physics.

deterministic Describes a system or model that allows for no randomness. Given the same starting condition and inputs, a deterministic system will always return the same output.

electricity A form of energy resulting from the existence of charged particles (such as electrons or protons).

electromagnetic spectrum The range of wavelengths or frequencies over which electromagnetic radiation extends.

electron A negatively charged particle that orbits the nucleus of an atom.

fermion A category of elementary particles.

finite Having limits or bounds.

Heisenberg uncertainty principle A scientific principle that states that it is impossible to measure both the position and the momentum of a quantum at the same time.

infinitesimal Extremely small.

interference The effect of two waves meeting, causing alternating areas of increased and decreased amplitude.

joule A unit of work or energy equal to the work done by a force of one newton acting through a distance of one meter.

macroscopic Large enough to be visible to the naked eye.

nuclear fission A reaction that occurs when neutrons bombard an atom of uranium and split its nucleus in half and release its contents. The result is the creation of a new barium and the release of significant amounts of energy.

photon A quantum of light.

portmanteau A word blending the sounds and combining the meanings of two other words.

probabilistic Describes a system or model that allows for randomness. Given the same starting condition and inputs, a probabilistic system can return a range of outputs.

quantize To divide into small but measurable increments

quantum (plural **quanta**) Any of the very small units into which many forms of matter or energy are subdivided.

quantum entanglement Occurs when two quanta become joined together and behave in a highly correlated manner.

quantum jump Occurs when an electron orbiting a nucleus instantaneously jumps from one orbit to another.

quantum state The form or position of a quantum.

quantum tunneling Occurs when a particle escapes the inside of a nucleus despite lacking adequate energy to do so.

qubit In quantum computing, the quantum equivalent of a bit. All data in a quantum computer is encoded into qubits.

quiddity Whatever makes something what it is.

subatomic particle A particle, such as a proton, neutron, or electron, that exists inside an atom.

superposition The notion that a quantum can exist in multiple states at the same time.

thermodynamics The branch of physical science that deals with the relations between heat and other forms of energy (such as mechanical, electrical, or chemical energy), and, by extension, of the relationships between all forms of energy.

transistor A type of semiconductor device that generates, controls, and amplifies an electrical signal.

wave function A list of all possible values for the position and momentum of a quantum system.

wave-particle duality The ability of a quantum to behave like both a wave and a particle.

Further Information

BOOKS

Ford, Kenneth W. *The Quantum World: Quantum Physics for Everyone*. Cambridge, MA: Harvard University Press, 2009.

Hobson, Art. *Tales of the Quantum: Understanding Physics' Most Fundamental Theory*. Oxford, UK: Oxford University Press, 2017.

McEvoy, J. P., and Oscar Zarate. *Introducing Quantum Theory: A Graphic Guide to Science's Most Puzzling Discovery*. London: Icon Books, 2014.

Orzel, Chad. *How to Teach Quantum Physics to Your Dog*. London: Oneworld Publications, 2010.

Susskind, Leonard, and Art Friedman. *Quantum Mechanics: The Theoretical Minimum*. New York: Basic Books, 2014.

WEBSITES

The Feynman Lectures on Physics
http://www.feynmanlectures.caltech.edu

This website makes available several lectures by a famed quantum physicist named Richard Feynman.

Phys.org
https://phys.org/physics-news/quantum-physics

Keep up with the latest news in the field of quantum physics here. In addition to news on topics in quantum physics, readers will find accessible articles on various other science topics.

Physics.org
http://www.physics.org

Let this website, maintained by the Institute of Physics, be your guide to physics resources on the web.

The Physics Classroom
http://www.physicsclassroom.com

The website enables users to access tutorials that relate to physics. The interactives section includes physics simulations and game-like challenges.

Bibliography

"A Theory of Everything." PBS.org, accessed February 18, 2018. http://www.pbs.org/faithandreason/intro/purpotoe-body.html.

Ball, Philip. "Why There Might Be Many More Universes Besides Our Own." BBC, March 21, 2016. http://www.bbc.com/earth/story/20160318-why-there-might-be-many-more-universes-besides-our-own.

Bosma, Wayne B. "Quantum Chemistry." Chemistry Explained, accessed February 16, 2018. http://www.chemistryexplained.com/Pr-Ro/Quantum-Chemistry.html.

Byrne, Peter. "The Many Worlds of Hugh Everett." *Scientific American*, October 21, 2008. https://www.scientificamerican.com/article/hugh-everett-biography.

Duff, Michael. "Theory of Everything: The Big Questions in Physics." *New Scientist*, June 1, 2011. https://www. newscientist.com/article/mg21028152-200-theory-of-everything-the-big-questions-in-physics.

Farmelo, Graham. "Churchill and the Bomb." Institute for Advanced Study, 2013. https://www.ias.edu/ ideas/2013/farmelo-churchill.

———. *The Strangest Man: The Hidden Life of Paul Dirac, Mystic of the Atom*. New York: Basic Books, 2009.

Finkbeiner, Ann. "Looking for Neutrinos, Nature's Ghost Particles." Smithsonian, November 2010. https://www. smithsonianmag.com/science-nature/looking-for-neutrinos-natures-ghost-particles-64200742.

Fölsing, Albrecht. *Albert Einstein: A Biography*. Translated by Ewald Osers. New York: Viking, 1997.

Gregersen, Eric. *The Britannica Guide to Relativity and Quantum Mechanics*. New York: Rosen Publishing Group, 2011.

Hawking, Stephen. *The Grand Design*. New York: Bantam Books, 2010.

Hay, Anthony J. G., and Patrick Walters. *The New Quantum Universe*. Cambridge, UK: Cambridge University Press, 2003.

Hobson, Art. *Tales of the Quantum*. Oxford, UK: Oxford University Press, 2017.

Holton, William Coffeen. "Quantum Computer." *Encyclopædia Britannica*, May 12, 2015. https://www.britannica.com/technology/quantum-computer.

Howell, Elizabeth. "Einstein's Theory of Special Relativity." Space.com, March 30, 2017. https://www.space.com/36273-theory-special-relativity.html.

Isaacson, Walter. "The World Needs More Rebels Like Einstein." *Wired*, April 1, 2007. https://www.*wired*.com/2007/04/the-world-needs-more-rebels-like-einstein/.

Kaplan, Sarah. "Quantum Entanglement, Science's 'Spookiest' Phenomenon, Achieved in Space." *Washington Post*, June 15, 2017. https://www.washingtonpost.com/news/speaking-of-science/wp/2017/06/15/quantum-entanglement-sciences-spookiest-phenomenon-achieved-in-space/?utm_term=.744843dd7847.

Krauss, Lawrence M. "A Blip that Speaks to Our Place in the Universe." *New York Times*, July 9, 2012. http://www.nytimes.com/2012/07/10/science/in-higgs-discovery-a-celebration-of-our-human-capacity.html?pagewanted=all.

Leibniz, G. W. *The Principles of Philosophy Known as Monadology*. Translated by Robert Latta. Oxford, UK: The Clarendon Press, 1898.

Moskowitz, Clara. "6 Implications of Finding a Higgs Boson Particle." Live Science, March 14, 2013. https://www.livescience.com/27893-higgs-boson-implications.html.

Orzel, Chad. "Six Things Everyone Should Know About Quantum Physics." *Forbes*, July 8, 2015. https://www.*forbes*.com/sites/chadorzel/2015/07/08/six-things-everyone-should-know-about-quantum-physics/#20020f6a7d46

Pais, Abraham. *Niels Bohr's Times, in Physics, Philosophy and Polity*. Oxford, UK: Clarendon Press, 1991.

Perkowitz, Sidney. "Relativity." *Encyclopædia Britannica*, November 21, 2017. https://www.britannica.com/ science/relativity.

Phillips, Lee. "The Never-Ending Conundrums of Classical Physics." Ars Technica, August 4, 2014. https://arstechnica.com/science/2014/08/the-never- ending-conundrums-of-classical-physics.

Powell, Devin. "What Is Quantum Cryptography?" *Popular Science*, March 3, 2016. https://www.popsci. com/what-is-quantum-cryptography.

Riordan, Michael. "Transistor: Electronics." *Encyclopædia Britannica*, January 3, 2018. https://www.britannica. com/technology/transistor.

Silver, Katie. "Will We Ever Have a Theory of Everything?" BBC, April 8, 2015. http://www.bbc.com/earth/ story/20150409-can-science-ever-explain-everything.

Spyrou, Artemis, and Wolfgang Mittig. "The Science Behind the First Nuclear Chain Reaction, Which Ushered in the Atomic Age 75 Years Ago." *Smithsonian Magazine*, December 1, 2017. https://www. smithsonianmag.com/innovation/the-science-behind- first-nuclear-chain-reaction-180967375/.

Thomson, J. J. "Cathode Rays." *Philos. Mag.* 44 (1897): 293.

Weinberg, Steven. "The Trouble with Quantum Mechanics." *New York Review of Books*, January 19, 2017. http://www.nybooks.com/articles/2017/01/19/ trouble-with-quantum-mechanics.

Williams, L. Pearce. "Michael Faraday: British Physicist and Chemist." *Encyclopædia Britannica*, October 18, 2017. https://www.britannica.com/biography/ Michael-Faraday.

Wolfram, Stephen. *A New Kind of Science*. Champaign, IL: Wolfram Media, 2002.

Index

About the Author

Kate Shoup has written more than forty books and has edited hundreds more. When not working, Shoup loves to travel, watch IndyCar racing, ski, read, and ride her motorcycle. She lives in Indianapolis with her husband, her daughter, and their dog.